WHEN THE GOING
GETS TOUGH

WHEN THE GOING GETS TOUGH

A FRAMEWORK FOR MEDICAL ERROR SURVIVORS

BERENDA SAYADOF

NEW DEGREE PRESS

WHEN THE GOING GETS TOUGH

A Framework For Medical Error Survivors

ISBN   978-1-64137-310-4   *Paperback*

          978-1-64137-600-6   *Ebook*

*For my family; my anchor
who always believes.*

*And for survivors of medical
error—wherever life
plants you, bloom with
grace.*

CONTENTS

INTRODUCTION   11

CHAPTER 1.   REAL TALK   27
CHAPTER 2.   IGNORANCE ISN'T ALWAYS BLISS   41
CHAPTER 3.   A COMPLEX SYSTEM   55
CHAPTER 4.   WHEN TRAGEDY STRIKES   63
CHAPTER 5.   GRIEF   79
CHAPTER 6.   FORGIVENESS   91
CHAPTER 7.   THE OTHER SIDE   105
CHAPTER 8.   THE DOMINO EFFECT   121
CHAPTER 9.   STRENGTH AND VULNERABILITY   139
CHAPTER 10. NEW MINDSET   157

ACKNOWLEDGEMENTS   171
WORKS REFERENCED   175

"to love life, to love it even
when you have no stomach for it
and everything you've held dear
crumbles like burnt paper in your hands,
your throat filled with the silt of it.
When grief sits with you, its tropical heat
thickening the air, heavy as water
more fit for gills than lungs;
when grief weights you like your own flesh
only more of it, an obesity of grief,
you think, How can a body withstand this?
Then you hold life like a face
between your palms, a plain face,
no charming smile, no violet eyes,
and you say, yes, I will take you
I will love you, again."

— ELLEN BASS

INTRODUCTION

"Make up your mind that no matter what comes your way, no matter how difficult, no matter how unfair, you will do more than simply survive. You will thrive in spite of it."

—JOEL OSTEEN

In 1995, a few days after being born, Cal Sheridan was mildly jaundiced.

This is usually typical of newborns, so it raised no concerns for Cal's doctors. However, Sue Sheridan's motherly intuition knew something was just not right. Three days after being born, Cal showed physical symptoms of extreme drowsiness and lethargy, and her husband Patrick caught on as well. She reported these alarming symptoms to the hospital, but her worries were dismissed because of her "new mom" status.

Sue still couldn't shake her intuition, so she immediately took Cal to the pediatrician's office the next day. The pediatrician told Sue what she'd already heard from previous doctors about the expectancy of jaundice arising in newborns and that there was no need for concern.

Cal soon turned a yellow-orange colour that really troubled Sue, and no one seemed to listen.

The culprit? Bilirubin.

Bilirubin is a yellow-orange compound naturally produced by the liver, but since newborns' livers aren't mature enough, bilirubin can accumulate and develop serious brain damage if the issue is not detected and treated early on.

This was the case for Cal. The symptoms that Sue was worried about were symptoms of high bilirubin levels, and even so, she kept being dismissed. A bilirubin test could have been administered on several occasions, both in the hospital and at the pediatrician's office, but these were not done.

Cal was again admitted on day five, and a bilirubin test was finally administered. Despite the alarming bilirubin levels, doctors were still not concerned and treated him with only phototherapy, which uses a special light to lower bilirubin levels in newborns. An exchange transfusion, which transfuses new blood into the body, should have been done but never was. Soon afterward, Cal began showing more serious physical symptoms, like body arching and trembling.

Cal did not respond to the phototherapy, and his symptoms only worsened to respiratory distress, neck arching, and high pitched crying, all textbook cases of the onset of Kernicterus, a type of brain damage that can be caused by high bilirubin levels.

The Sheridans then requested an MRI scan to be taken of Cal's brain because he was showing such distressing symptoms. When the scan came back, the parents were told that the results were "insignificant."

In her blog for the Centers For Disease (CFD), Sue writes, "Little did I know that my newborn son was suffering brain damage before my eyes and in my arms. I will be haunted by that memory [forever]."[1]

When Cal was eighteen months, Sue got her hands on a copy of the MRI that was taken of Cal at five days old. She then

---

1   "Cal Sheridan's Journey With Jaundice And Kernicterus | CDC". 2018. *Centers For Disease Control And Prevention.*

sought a diagnosis from a team of specialists in another state and found out the report had **actually indicated abnormalities in certain parts of his brain that were originally read as "insignificant."**

Cal was diagnosed with classic, textbook Kernicterus at eighteen months.

Sue and Patrick had no option but to file a lawsuit. After seven years of litigation, the Sheridans settled.

Eighteen months.

It took the system eighteen months for Cal to be eventually diagnosed with Kernicterus and given treatment, but irreversible damages were already done.

He has athetoid cerebral palsy throughout his body, neurosensory hearing loss, enamel dysplasia on his front teeth, crossed eyes, and other abnormalities.

As a result of late diagnosis, Cal currently lives with significant cerebral palsy.

***

Like Sue, many other lives have been impacted due to human and medical error. In Canada, one patient dies every 13 minutes and 14 seconds due to the same adverse events.[2] In the US, the 2017 Institute for Healthcare Improvement (IHI) report shows us that out of the 2,536 patients who took the IHI medical error survey, sixty-three percent of patients disclosed that they were not informed of the medical error they experienced.[3] And this is just a snapshot.

When patients distrust their health care providers, they may seek out alternative forms of traditional medicine. Some people swear they will never go back to a certain family physician because she/he doesn't listen enough, while others may fall into a conspiracy that politics are to blame for the whole health care fiasco. Some people even turn to homeopathy, naturopathy, or Chinese/Oriental medicine as a more trusting health care option.

Others just give up altogether—and something must be done about this.

---

2   RiskAnalytica. "The Case for Investing in Patient Safety in Canada." (2017).

3   NORC at the University of Chicago and IHI/NPSF Lucian Leape Institute. "Americans' Experiences with Medical Errors and Views on Patient Safety". 2017 *NORC at the University of Chicago and IHI/ NPSF Lucian Leape Institute.*

I've come across two terms that have been used interchangeably to describe patients who have experienced medical error: a "victim" and a "survivor". I see a victim of medical error as someone whose life has ended because of that error—like a medication mix-up, preventable surgical failure, or a late/misdiagnosis. These patients fell victim to a faulty system and, unfortunately, did not make it out the other side to tell their own story.

On the other hand, although survivors have suffered a traumatic medical error, they are *still here* to tell their stories. At times, we all forget to appreciate the mere fact that we are alive, yet being alive is the first step needed to make a difference in this world.

Even so, the ability to live is prematurely taken away from some patients. If you are reading this book as someone who has experienced a traumatic medical error, you've survived and your story is only the beginning of an uplifting journey ahead.

With medical error, it's hard to pinpoint an exact source, because while the causes could have been the fault of an *individual* health care provider, it's not always thoroughly acknowledged that medical error can result from the entire system's failure as a whole.

This is not to overlook the fact that health care front-line staff, like doctors, nurses, and surgeons, can (and do) make their own, isolated mistakes that cost lives. However, not seeing past these front-line staff feeds into ignorance.

Ignorance can lead to false generalizations from patients, which starves the improvement of our health care system and prevents smart actions from being made that can actually create a difference in medicine.

After all, as patients, we put the *patient* in *patient safety*.

One of the biggest misconceptions I've seen from patients, including medical error survivors, is that we are powerless in changing the health care system. Before I wrote this book, I was often frustrated by how hopeless I felt in protecting my own health. I felt I was essentially placing my life into the hands of individuals working for a bigger system that kept making mistakes, one I was not allowed to tackle because... hey, I'm just one person against an entire world of professionals and policymakers.

Besides, *what could I even do?*

However, while doing patient safety research, I came to believe something else.

I've learned that the best way to improve the system is to be part of the solution, even if the journey will be one of the hardest things you'll ever experience.

The idea that we can't make an impact is beyond false. Time and time again, patients (and health care providers) have shown that one person can make big dents in the health care system—all it takes is speaking up and talking to the right people.

Since Cal's diagnosis with cerebral palsy, Sue has been avidly advocating for patient safety. Sue's story began when she reached out to parents of children with Kernicterus, and she and seven other moms got together with one simple goal in mind: to make a change.

In her twenty-plus years of advocating, Sue has testified before Congress in Washington, DC, been recruited by the government, and has even worked with national and international health organizations like the World Health Organization.

She brought together mothers, policymakers, researchers, accreditors, public health officials, and politicians to partner to implement change. After years of hard work, Sue and the other stakeholders were influential in changing the Academy of Pediatrics guidelines on Bilirubin tests. In 2004, the guidelines were updated to raise awareness on high levels of bilirubin, and in 2009, the guidelines were updated to include the recommendation of universal predischarge bilirubin screening in the States.

Sue proved that one person can absolutely make a change, even after experiencing so much tragedy. Sue couldn't save Cal from Kernicterus, but she could save the *next* Cal.

However, in the midst of Cal's medical journey, Sue's husband Patrick suffered a medical error as well.

In 1999, a mass was found in Patrick's spine and diagnosed as benign, so the Sheridans tracked down one of the best neurosurgeons in the nation and got the tumor surgically removed.

A pathologist examined a frozen sample of the mass and then informed the operating room (O.R.) facility.

O.R. understood the results were benign, but the pathologist "believed it to be very suspicious and ordered more stains to further define the tumor," Sue explains in an interview with The Agency for Healthcare Research & Quality (AHRQ)[4].

The stain results came back to the pathologist, and **cancer was indeed detected**. The final pathology report was sent to

4   "Sue Sheridan Video On Patient Safety." Agency for Healthcare Research & Quality. 2012.

the surgeon but "was either filed without the surgeon ever seeing it, got lost, or was misplaced" Sue explains.[5]

The cancer went untreated for six months because of this miscommunication.

It had invaded Patrick's spinal cord, and in 2002, he died due to the aggressiveness of the cancer.

"Both Cal's and Pat's errors are examples of simple, yet catastrophic systems failure due to communication breakdowns and uncoordinated teamwork"[6]

—SUE SHERIDAN

The Sheridan's medical error experience demonstrates that patient safety could go absolutely wrong in *all* dimensions. Even so, one person can still make the last call rather than allowing painful memories and trauma to drown her.

Sue could have given up and grieved forever. She could have chosen to live in resentment and not have gotten a word out to the world about her situation. If she hadn't gone public,

---

5   Ibid.
6   Ibid

other moms wouldn't have known about her story and none of the change she helped create could have happened.

**

Sue's story introduced me to the world of patient safety through her role in the documentary, "To Err Is Human", which highlights her family's story and their traumatic journey.

I was studying in my last year at Queen's in Kingston, Ontario and was part of a Practical Experience program to test the waters of public health careers. I attended a keynote talk by Dr. Paul Bowie who played "To Err is Human." After the documentary ended, I remember sitting back in my seat and looking around to see if everyone else was as dumbfounded about the medical error as I was.

This is happening here in North America? I thought.

I realized in that moment that I was actually a "noob" sitting among professionals in the health care field—doctors, nurses, professors, and administrators.

I was frustrated that it took me four years into my science university degree to learn that patients are harmed so much more than you think in developed countries. And even more so, that I wouldn't even have found out if I hadn't specifically sought out a patient safety seminar.

"Someone needs to write a book on all these patients and the pain they go through because of medical harm", I said to my mom over the phone as I walked home that night, and that someone ended up being me a year later.

I discovered a newfound passion the second I finished watching "To Err Is Human", one that completely changed the course of my studies and future career path. I instantly engulfed myself in patient safety books, reading about theories and dynamics surrounding complex health care systems.

I started off as a "nobody" in this field, but in the months leading up to writing this book, I vowed to teach myself everything and anything related to patient safety. I spoke with professionals in the field, like professors, CEOs, and physicians, to gain their perspective on what goes on behind the scenes of patient safety. More importantly, I spoke with as many patients who have survived medical error as I could— both well – and lesser-known.

Over time, I realized that the patients who were not only the strongest but also the most productive in changing the system followed a particular framework that allowed them to process their experiences more effectively than others.

While there's no one-step formula with emotional journeys like medical error, I have come up with a simple foundation to start with.

***

"Human progress is neither automatic nor inevitable...Every step toward the goal of justice requires sacrifice, suffering, and struggle." Martin Luther King, Jr.

Courage is defined as strength in the face of pain or grief— and I've found that everyone who has made an impact in patient safety, both patients and health care providers, embraced vulnerability on a level too frightening for most people to embrace. To "make a change" in a health care system so complex and multi-dimensional requires the first step of speaking up. Telling policymakers to make it a rule for all babies to be tested for Kernicterus when you're a single mom with only a small team of other moms supporting you is difficult—but also courageous.

In my interview with her, Sue told me that *many* policymakers shut her down because she didn't have the credentials to make bold statements about the US health care system, and yet her one voice had the final say.

Situations that "just aren't fair" can, no doubt, be deeply painful. Not only are you left dealing with the unjust actions toward you, but you feel like no one is listening. It's human nature to build walls and not trust people from the system because of that one person who wronged you—but I've found the individuals best at dealing with unfortunate situations are those willing to let their guards down and listen.

They educate themselves about the "opposing team", they listen to the ones who have wronged them, and they work toward a greater good.

For anyone who has survived grave medical harm, this book is dedicated to you—whether you have lost loved ones because of medical error or carry the direct burden on yourself. If you work in the public health system, this book is also for you. My aim is to raise awareness on patient stories and on the bigger, most important, health care picture—a patient-centered world.

Patients need partnerships from health care systems, and health care systems need partnerships from patients—I've found the two to go hand-in-hand perfectly and you'll see it through the patient stories I share in my book.

Any hardships medical error survivors experience can be an exemplar for the health care system of what *not* to do.

I love the saying, "When the going gets tough, the tough get going." It's the perfect way to express the courage and strength needed after a difficult situation, but it also shows us that our story is just beginning after any seemingly debilitating life event.

This book encompasses a variety of stories, both from patients and health care practitioners, in hopes of providing you with a sense of belonging among a whole community of survivors, making your situation slightly more bearable than just thinking you are alone in this journey.

More importantly, you, as a medical error survivor, will be left empowered.

Survivors outlined in this book show that their story didn't stop at the harm they experienced. Anger can make someone do many things that seem like the right options in the moment, but they only bring temporary healing. We can choose to use our anger as fuel where it matters most in the long term.

This book is designed to walk you through the confusing times of dealing with medical harm and give you an alternative view of the health care system besides the misconception that the whole system is the "bad guy."

My book consists of three parts:

- Understanding health care systems
- Hearing patient and physician stories
- Taking action

My dearest readers, I hope this book empowers you to handle your medical error grief in a new light—one that introduces you to an entire world of patient safety and hope for a more improved system ahead.

CHAPTER 1:

REAL TALK

Before I take off my own rose-colored glasses and start a blunt discussion on the failures of our health care system and global views as a whole, I want us to keep in mind how important it is to count our blessings.

Many other countries have the shorter end of the health care stick, like Central African Republic, and Myanmar, and Sierra Leone, whose health care systems fall in the bottom 3 ranks out of the 191 countries assessed in the World Health Organization (WHO) health systems performance report in 2000.[7] It's important to be mindful that developed countries like the United States and Canada, at the very least, have big organizations that more productively stand behind patients

---

7   World Health Organization. *The World Health Report 2000 – Health systems: Improving Performance.* 2000.

and fight for safer health care systems, like The Commonwealth Fund.

The Commonwealth Fund is a private American foundation that mandates for patient safety and supports research behind improving health care systems. This nonprofit organization conducted a study in 2017, ranking eleven developed countries by the quality of their health care systems.

This intricate study looked at five key factors in each health care system: care process, access, administrative efficiency, equity, and health care outcomes. Canada and the US were assessed, along with Australia, France, the UK, and six other countries. **Of the eleven developed countries assessed in the study, Canada ranked ninth and the US ranked last in health care quality.**[8] All five of the factors studied were also ranked individually, and Canada and the US still failed to make the top five countries for those categories.[9]

If we look at these statistics, Canada and the US are doing pretty bad compared to many other developed countries.

---

8   Doty, Michelle M., David Squires, Dana O. Sarnak, Eric C. Schneider, and Arnav Shah. "Mirror, Mirror 2017: International Comparison Reflects Flaws and Opportunities for Better U.S. Health Care." *The Commonwealth Fund*, 2017.

9   Doty, Michelle M., David Squires, Dana O. Sarnak, Eric C. Schneider, and Arnav Shah. "Mirror, Mirror 2017: International Comparison Reflects Flaws and Opportunities for Better U.S. Health Care." *The Commonwealth Fund*, 2017.

Health care is not a competition, but studies like this one aim to understand why North American countries like the US and Canada, so-called "developed countries," ranked so poorly compared to the UK and Australia, which ranked first and second, respectively.

In a perfect world, our governments would look at this data and create immediate concrete steps to better the dynamics of our system, but creating a patient-centered world is a movement, and as with all movements, it cannot be formed overnight.

The danger of comparing health care systems is that the state of a health care system can become subjective.

According to The Commonwealth Fund, Canada and the US are struggling with their health care quality compared to nine other countries. In comparison, the 2000 WHO health systems performance report suggests that Canada's health care system placed 30 out of 190 countries and the US placed 37. In this sense, we're doing quite well![10]

So which is it? Are we doing well or not?

---

10 World Health Organization. *The World Health Report 2000 – Health systems: Improving Performance.* 2000.

While comparative studies are so crucial in helping us understand what makes a productive health care system, they can also be the silent culprits behind the global stereotype that all developed countries, like the US and Canada, have exemplary health care systems.

If we stop comparing our health care systems to other countries for one brief moment, we will suddenly start hearing the loud cries of patients all over the States and Canada affected by failures from our health care systems, which the rest of the world sees as "pretty good" compared to what else is going on globally.

Subjective comparisons stop patient safety from becoming a priority and turn it into a privilege. Some might say, "Well, Canada is a lot better off than the Sierra Leone—at least you actually have access to advanced medicine or trained professionals." True...but no matter how developed or undeveloped a country is, asking for patient safety movements shouldn't be seen as a privilege or a "first-world problem."

Patient safety should be a basic right, which is why our responsibility is to strive for a safer health care system globally, whether we are Canadian, American, or Sierra Leonean.

When I started brainstorming ideas for this book, I remember being set on making it all about patient safety and medical error. However, I soon came to realize that simply saying "I want to write a book on patient safety" is like saying, "I want to write a book on rocks," or on the entire universe and beyond.

Where would those books start and where would they end? What could you possibly say before those "books" turned into textbooks?

The nature of patient safety is just like that—it's an abyss. I realized that a more productive step would be to focus on a smaller aspect of patient safety rather than face the entirety head-on.

That's why it's so crucial for patient safety advocates to get out of the "all or nothing" mindset. It would be great if we could help improve *all the* system's failures, but by having a generalized goal, we tend to oversee the little, important details that will get us *to* the bigger picture.

THE SWISS CHEESE MODEL

Picture this: You're an aircraft manufacturer in charge of assembling a plane's engines.

Your last task is to attach propellers to the engines so the propellers *just* fit the engine and can rotate smoothly. You finally finish but don't notice (or maybe you do) that you accidentally fused the propeller of one of the engines to the engine wall. Instead of propelling as it should, the propeller is permanently stuck in one place. However, you've always trusted the testing crew that comes in after you to notice and fix any errors because they test-run the planes and it's their job to find mistakes.

The next day, the testing crew takes the plane for a spin around the block and the plane flies smoothly without an issue—somehow the mistake you made didn't show initial signs of danger and passed the flying test—and now the plane is ready to be used by airlines *which millions of people have faith in.*

Take note that the one error made it through *two* manufacturing steps without anyone noticing.

It's easy to think big mistakes like that will be caught, and an obvious engine mistake is sure to be spotted somewhere along the line before the plane is actually used in the real world.

But what if the mistake is not so obvious? What if others in the plane manufacturing field are making similar, small mistakes and the company goes on producing faulty planes, all the while millions of lives are in danger?

The Swiss Cheese Model of Accident Causation—developed by James Reason, a professor in psychology—gives us a deeper look into the complexity of the systems in charge of our health and how blaming individual doctors or nurses simply won't cut it.[11]

The Swiss Cheese Model explains that every moment of contact patients have with the health care system, both direct and indirect, acts as one layer of Swiss cheese, and as we all know, Swiss cheese has holes in it.[12]

Say a patient has five interactions with the health care system. There are now hypothetically five layers of cheese assigned to this one patient's medical history.

Reason's model illustrates these slices of cheese stacked side by side, each with their own unique holes. According to the model, for most medical errors to occur, a hole's size and location on one slice aligns with a similar hole on the rest of the slices, and a medical error can now "leak" through every slice—i.e., through every level of patient interaction.[13]

---

11 Reason, James. "Human Error: Models And Management". *BMJ* 320 (2000): 768-770.
12 Ibid.
13 Ibid.

The alignment increases the chance for an error to go through the first slice and make its way to the last slice, or throughout various levels of health care system management.

Imagine instead of one hole aligning, suddenly multiple holes align at different slices, which invites more errors to pass through the slices...that's our system right there.

While my airplane analogy is a completely made-up story and quite exaggerated, the essence is real and very frightening.

In my analogy, the engine propeller mistake found its way through the "Swiss cheese holes" until the plane made it out to the other side, bringing the grave error along with it and instantly magnifying its chances of crashing.

Models like these, and years of research behind medical errors, show us how much more complex our system is to even fathom. So while your first instinct is to figure out what went wrong in the way you were treated medically, and why you had to endure the trauma, it's important to truly understand the beast that our system(s) is.

ASSUMPTIONS, ASSUMPTIONS, ASSUMPTIONS

Early in 2019, I was chatting with a professor from Queen's University, Dr. Rylan Egan, who has a background in Educational Psychology and has worked in Quality Improvement initiatives.

My goal was to confront my stubborn belief that one problem with medical error is that medical school students simply aren't being taught enough about medical error. I was set on the harsh assumption that our medical students are not screened enough to go out in the real world—which doesn't consist of textbook case studies and grades.

This encounter made me realize how important it is important to educate oneself with facts rather than assumptions.

I asked Dr. Egan to briefly explain the curriculum that goes behind a residency in Canada and post-graduate work at Queen's to get a better, unbiased idea of what is actually going on.

He said the problem is a lot deeper than just "teaching patient safety." First, Canada's resident programs have been evolving and their student assessment methods have advanced to a level that screens for patient safety skills a lot more than previous years—and he's right.

By 2020, all of Canada's residency schools will take on an improved Competency-Based Medical Education (CBME) model to ensure students are getting more optimized skill sets before entering their specialized careers.[14]

Studies are showing us that as the years go by, new doctors *are* becoming more equipped to provide quality health care because of constant improvements in technology and curriculum, such as CBME.[15]

A study from the Harvard T. H. Chan School of Public Health in Boston evaluated whether the longevity of patients is affected by the age of physicians.

Between 2011 and 2014, they randomly sampled 736,000 American Medicare patients ages 65 and up who received care from 18,854 hospital physicians around age of forty-one.[16]

The researchers looked at several results, including patient readmissions and deaths within the first thirty days of the

---

14 "Residents 'Learn the Ropes' of Competence by Design." Dalhousie University.

15 "Competency-Based Medical Education." The Canadian Association of Pathologists (Association canadienne des pathologistes).

16 Tsugawa, Yusuke, Joseph P Newhouse, Alan M Zaslavsky, Daniel M Blumenthal, and Anupam B Jena. 2017. "Physician Age And Outcomes In Elderly Patients In Hospital In The US: Observational Study". *BMJ* no. 357.

hospital visits. They found that younger physicians had fewer patient mortality rates than older physicians.

This is not to discredit experienced, older physicians but simply to highlight that advancements *are* being made...just a little slower than we'd all like.

Dr. Yusuke Tsugawa, the author of that study, said in a CBC News segment that:

> A lot of patients have a perception that older doctors give a better quality of care. But previous studies—multiple studies—have shown that younger doctors have more aptitude.[17]

Dr. Tsugawa continued to explain:

> Medical technologies are evolving all the time and it might be harder for older doctors to keep up with the evidence. New guidelines are updated every five to ten years. Newer doctors train based on the newest evidence and skills and technologies. Therefore, [new physicians] may be more up-to-date when they start providing care.[18]

---

17 Marcus, Mary. "Does Your Doctor's Age Matter?" *CBS News,* 2017.
18 Ibid.

Now, my argument of "medical school students aren't being trained enough" changed to the question of "so if the problem isn't curriculum, what is?"

I learned the issue is indeed a lot more complex than simply making assumptions that place blame on health care providers or making generalizations about our health care system.

My chat with Dr. Egan took an unexpected turn because after instantly dropping my very wrong assumption about medical school students, I found myself explaining how stuck I felt not knowing where to begin helping our health care system.

"Where do you even start?" I asked, and his response threw me for an even bigger loop, which was just what I needed.

He said, "There isn't a system. There are a million systems. It's like saying we have one blood system in our bodies. We have millions of blood systems."

Long past my interview with him, Dr. Egan's words kept repeating themselves to me, serving as a reminder that the system is indeed way more complex than you or I or even experts can fathom.

So many systems intertwine in a hospital—or any medical setting, for that matter—that it's near impossible for someone to pinpoint exactly where an error occurred and how to track its movements.

Similar to the infinite nature of outer space, where do we start if we're only looking at the bigger picture and trying to comprehend everything all at once? Patient safety is the best example of why starting small will go a long, long way, and this is exactly where you come in.

Cue your entrance

CHAPTER 2:

IGNORANCE ISN'T ALWAYS BLISS

––––

Before I researched the world of patient safety, I thought the solution to patient harm was quite clear: Doctors need to stop making mistakes—plain and simple.

I always wondered how health care providers could take on a job that carries so much responsibility and continue to make mistakes left and right.

Growing up in Canada, I heard many stories from my family and friends about things like doctors prescribing them medication that didn't seem to fix their health concerns or their experiences of borderline neglect from physicians. This went on for years until I started becoming more independent and naturally formed the belief that our health care system isn't as good as it's hyped up to be. I believed I shouldn't trust doctors' judgments as much as they want us to.

But one particular interaction I had with a minor medication error in the summer of 2018 made my subtle resentment not so subtle, and I became vocally skeptical of doctors and the entire health care system.

In 2018, I experienced back-to-back cold and flu episodes due to stress from school, a mediocre diet at best, and the refusal to get a flu shot.

Through the years of my biology degree, and after countless courses on health and genetics, I became a real health nut—trying unsuccessful hard-core sugar-free diets and lecturing people on the importance of a balanced gut flora.

In my "flu season" phase, I became adamant about not taking antibiotics unnecessarily, all the while being pressured by my mom to get prescribed some just to "get my flu over with."

It's a common belief that antibiotics are the fast lane to recovery from flu because that's just a tempting belief—they have the word *anti* in them, so they must be this magical medication that *anti*s germs away, right?

Not really. Antibiotics target bacterial cells, mainly found in infections. Viral cells in viruses like the flu are shaped differently from bacterial cells, which is why most viruses can't be broken down by antibiotics. Taking them when you have a virus and not a bacterial infection can do more harm than good. First, antibiotics can deplete your good gut bacteria and create an imbalance in your gut flora (no thanks). This is the biggest reason I wanted to avoid them in the first place.

Second, the over-prescription of antibiotics is a real epidemic in our global public health system because bacteria can outsmart antibiotics over time and get more resilient, so we have to race to create antibiotics that out-strengthen bacteria. The Center for Disease Control and Prevention and other health care professionals have deemed antibiotics "one of the world's most pressing public health problems" because some bacteria have become resistant to the strongest antibiotics out there.[19] Over-prescription of antibiotics is a real crisis.

With all this knowledge of viruses in hand, I was determined even while I kept getting the flu—I wouldn't take antibiotics if I didn't need to. However, during a more severe bout of the flu that year, the physician thought I had strep throat and told me there wasn't "any way around recovering quickly without

19 "National Antimicrobial Resisance Monitoring System for Enteric Bacteria (NARMS)." *Centers for Disease Control and Prevention.*

antibiotics." While I'm stubborn about not taking antibiotics, I'm not stubborn enough to ignore my doctor's orders.

This truly felt like a betrayal of everything I stood for, but I trusted the physician's word for it—I had no other choice.

A week came and went, and my "strep throat" cleared up, but a few days later, I was bedridden for four days from the strongest wave of similar flu symptoms I had ever experienced.

I went back to the walk-in clinic, this time greeted by a resident student. Instead of relying on observational exams, he took a swab sample of my saliva and we only waited a short while for the results. He came back with the news that it wasn't strep throat and he couldn't prescribe me antibiotics.

He also said that I most likely **never had strep throat**. I asked him why I was given antibiotics when I could have gone without them. He reluctantly explained that sometimes tests aren't done for strep because the doctor has a lot of visual evidence at hand to make a call.

So essentially: I didn't have to take the antibiotics I was prescribed.

I. Was. Livid.

Since I am careful about what medication I take and the effects that medication can have on my body, that very moment made me the most skeptical I've ever been about the health care system.

I understand my situation might seem like an insignificant "medical error"—if you can call it that—compared to thousands of patients who experience near-death harm or even death itself. However, at that moment, **I felt like I had lost control of the safety of my health,** and I guarantee many of us feel this way when we experience medical errors, no matter how big or small.

NEGLECT ME NOT

It's a scary thing when the people in charge of maintaining our health leave us feeling neglected, but it's worse when they make us feel *we're* in the wrong.

I've become very familiar with the term gaslighting because I've seen it subtly happen to many of the medical error survivors I interviewed for this book. We often use the word 'gaslight' to describe the way one person in a relationship—be it romantic, business, or platonic—psychologically manipulates the other person by planting seeds of confusion and even doubt in their minds.

This doesn't always have to be intentional.

For starters, Sue Sheridan was dismissed multiple times in the first few days of Cal's birth because "she was a new mom" and there was no need to worry about Cal's skin discoloration.

In most instances of medical error, the patient *is* left feeling neglected, and while some hospitals are productive and cooperate with the patient after medical error, that is not always the case. Many times, as in Sue's case, the hospital turned from a safe haven for patients into what I like to call "a corporation." Lawyers protected the hospital and health care providers from lawsuit damages and the priority of cooperating with Sue as the patient was debunked.

***

You may also notice in later chapters that the real-life medical error stories are predominantly of women. In my nine months of research, I attempted to reach out to *any* patient who experienced a medical error, but only women responded. The stories I found online were predominantly of women as well.

This got me thinking about gender biases and stereotypes. Has society placed an unrealistic expectation on men that hinders them from stepping out as much as women on medical error? While my personal research doesn't fall under a proper scientific study by any means, I think gender biases can play a role in how much patients can speak up and be heard in our society.

If a stigma exists preventing men from speaking up, it's important to start this discussion. Research has found gender biases on women who experience medical errors, so there should be no surprise if men experience it too, which is all the more reason to help raise awareness on medical error.

The WomanStats Project is a research and database project that began in 2001. It contains one of the largest data compilations of women in the world, with over 310 variables spread across 174 countries. WomanStats aims to explore the safety of women around the world, and the WomanStats Blog is an offshoot project that raises awareness of important factors that affect a woman's life globally.

One article published by the WomanStats blog, titled *"Doctors Who Don't Listen: The Gaslighting Epidemic of Women,"* outlines a very real bias that female patients experience in medicine.

The article explains that, until 1990, medical trials were only run on men and their "symptoms and perceptions of pain."[20] Only after 1990 did the National Institutes of Health create the Office of Research on Women's Health, but medicine already had its traditions and policies set in place, which as with all traditions, are very hard to change.[21]

"Medical research suggests that estrogen changes female perception of pain and the response to painkillers, which implies that there are legitimate differences between how men and women perceive pain," the article explains.[22]

But when studies predominantly run on men have shown humans to have a certain level of perception of pain, and women suddenly spoke up saying otherwise, it's no surprise that the health care system would naturally be more inclined to believe scientific studies than to simply listen to the minority. "Doctors are diagnosing women based off of men's symptoms" and this only adds to the stigma that the different symptoms women experience are "more psychological," the blog explains.[23]

---

20 KM. "Doctors Who Don't Listen: The Gaslighting Epidemic of Women." Womansats Project, 2019.

21 Ibid.

22 Ibid.

23 Ibid.

"Female lives are at stake due to the biases about their inability to understand their own bodies"[24]

— WOMANSTATS BLOG

When I came across this blog, I reflected on my personal medical experiences. I remembered my short visit with a doctor in 2015 about a sudden onset of emotional mood swings that came around the same time I started taking a certain prescribed medication. I knew enough about my mental health to know that my mood swings were not usual, and they were most likely from the medication, so I told the male physician I wanted to stop taking them.

His response was definitely a subtle form of gaslighting. I remember him furrowing his brows and telling me that the medication shouldn't be causing any mood swings, and that science hasn't backed the association between extreme moodiness and that medication. He then prescribed me a refill of that very medication when I was there to tell him I didn't want to continue taking it any longer.

I didn't buy into it. The sudden intensity of my emotions that had started to affect my day-to-day life was telling me a different story than this physician. I followed up with another

---

24 KM. "Doctors Who Don't Listen: The Gaslighting Epidemic of Women." Womansats Project, 2019.

physician a few days later. She told me that other patients on that same medications had experienced similar symptoms, even though there was no direct scientific association between the two. So I stopped taking the medication immediately and happily went back to my "normal" self.

Gender biases are, unfortunately, present in our society in many ways, and they're most likely a result of decades and centuries of old-fashioned gender inequality and traditions set by men back when women had no say in policymaking.

Fortunately, since 1990, when women started being included in medical studies, our health care systems have been waking up to gender differences and the effect those differences have on the perception of pain and health symptoms.[25]

Even so, I want us to start the discussion on the quieter factors of medical error. Like gender inequality, I have heard about other types of neglect that can occur in medicine, like the neglect of the lesbian, gay, bisexual, and transgender (LGBT+) community and patients who suffer from mental illnesses. All these little factors have developed from old, wrong beliefs well before our time that can affect the way some patients are treated in medicine.

_____

25   Ibid.

National nonprofit organization Lambda Legal aims to raise awareness on the rights of LGBT+ and people living with HIV. With the help of one hundred other organizations, it conducted a survey from 4916 LGBT+ respondents on the quality of care they received in 2009.

The Lambda Legal summary report states:

Almost 8 percent of LGB respondents reported that they had outright been denied needed health care. [Almost 27 percent] of all transgender and gender-nonconforming respondents reported being denied care and 19 percent of respondents living with HIV also reported being denied care.[26]

The informative report also explained that 10 percent of the respondents experienced harsh language from their health care providers, and 11 percent reported that health care professionals refused to even touch them.[27]

The more we educate ourselves on these preventable factors, the more we can use our voice to partner with health care and make a change.

---

26 Lambda Legal. *When Health Care Isn't Caring: Lambda Legal's Survey on Discrimination Against LGBT People and People Living with HIV*. 2010.
27 Ibid.

When I started telling people I'm advocating for a patient-centered health care system, a few said to me, "Berenda, some health care practitioners won't be happy about you going after the health care system."

But I am not going after anyone. I am simply trying to raise awareness on preventable mistakes happening in our health care system that *can* be fixed with the help of amazing health care professionals and patients alike.

Some people definitely won't be happy about the bluntness of patient safety advocacy, because it challenges traditional views that have been in play for years. However, I've learned from patients who were successful in finding their voice in patient safety that while one or two health care providers were *not* willing to cooperate or hear what the patients had to say—double the number of health care providers, professors, organizations, and communities were willing to support the medical error survivors.

Proactive health care providers and hospitals *are* out there— those who are open-minded to listen to patients and become part of the ever-growing demand for patient safety. It's a matter of seeking your resources and selectively choosing which people will help you move toward your goal of making a difference.

Only when I started doing research for this book did my negative and angry view of our health care system start to turn around. I suddenly realized a majority of health care staff and educators are actually supportive in one's journey post-medical-error.

I had just been focusing on the 1 percent creating the disharmony. The irony of my resentment toward the health care system was that I was only hurting myself.

By educating myself, I gained a clearer understanding of what makes up medical error and I realized I had been allowing my fears of falling through the gaps of the system to *mislead* me in my views about doctors, nurses, and the overall dynamic of our health care system. This is the realization I encourage you to explore on your own time as we uncover medical error and patient stories together.

CHAPTER 3:

A COMPLEX SYSTEM

We sometimes get overwhelmed with big anythings—big projects, big exams, big decisions, big moves, big dreams.

The monster images we've created in our minds of "big" concepts or people make it seem impossible to go anywhere near them. Likewise, some might see the complexity of the health care system as a disheartening beast to unravel and improve, but I like to think otherwise.

When you're given such a diverse and multilayered system, it usually means many people are working in it.

You have your usual doctors, physicians, nurses, custodians, technicians, desk representatives, etc. working on-site in hospitals and clinical settings. Then you have the board of committees, presidents, vice presidents, volunteers, and patients working behind the scenes to help things run smoothly.

We don't stop there though. We have health ministries, politicians, mayors, representatives, etc. working behind the behind-the-scenes to cover the bigger picture stuff. Then we have big organizations like the United Nations and the World Health Organization working for the global health of populations, and the list keeps growing.

In other words: A complex system = many, many people to reach out to and speak with.

I used to look at the health care system and feel so overwhelmed with how I could find my place and help make improvements, but my journey of teaching myself about patient safety showed me I have pools of resources within an arm's reach. Today, especially, with social media, we can contact people we never would have dreamed of speaking with just by sending a single email.

Sometimes you only need one person in the world of health care to hear your story, because that one person knows someone else who can help you, and BOOM: your network to inspire and influence grows from there. Whether that one person is a fellow patient, neighbor, doctor, friend of a friend of a politician, a public speaker, or even a journalist—one person can help get you closer to the bigger picture.

It will surprise you to see that this "beast" of the health care system that we've been building up for ourselves is only human beings with title positions, years of expertise, and, for the most part, a willingness to help out.

If one person shuts you down, so be it. Go to the next. That's the beauty of our health care system because of all the layers that encompass it.

No matter what negative and painful event anyone goes through, there is always a silver lining. The death of a loved one, a life-changing accident, being in debt, living with addiction, experiencing rejection, being diagnosed with a life-threatening health condition—these are critical moments in your life where you can build a community of listeners and supporters.

Sue Sheridan built her community of seven other moms who experienced the same late-diagnosis battle she experienced with her son. Together, they got the attention of higher-ups.

When I spoke with Sue about how she and her group of moms went about making their way through such a complex health care system, she replied, "We moms were so naive to the health care system, which was really a gift. Because we didn't know the barriers, we didn't go into this thinking, 'We'll never do this.' We went into this thinking, 'We're going to make a change'."

We do not need to be experts in any field to be a part of the team and make our voices heard—we just need passion, which you develop when you decide you want to be part of a bigger movement.

Have you fallen victim to the system's gaps? **Yes**. Have you endured the physical, emotional, and mental toll the gaps created? **Yes**. Is it safe to say no one else in this world has the insight you have through your unique journey from the medical error? **Absolutely**—That's your key to making a change.

While you may have lost something, or someone, through medical error', you've also gained a very personal lens that only you can use to move one step closer to improving the system, not just for your own lifetime's sake, but for many others to come.

BLAME GAME

In his "Human Error" paper published in 2000, James Reason, the same researcher who developed the Swiss Cheese model, explains, "Blaming individuals is emotionally more satisfying than targeting institutions."[28]

But dare I say that blame isn't as worthwhile. It may seem easier to take legal action against an individual professional or confront them, but the problem will still lie deep in the system.

Generally speaking, it's our human nature to point fingers.

We can have a patient blaming the nurse for not being attentive enough, and then have a nurse blaming the physician for not communicating information effectively to them, when, in turn, the physician blames the nurse for doing certain tasks incorrectly. If this is the case, then The. Cycle. Will. Never. End.

The Institute for Health care Improvement highlighted a 2017 publication from the United Nations outlining a detailed analysis of the blame culture in UK incident reports.

Cooper J. and his team randomly selected incident reports of various levels of harm and associated each to a certain degree of blame. From 975 samples, family physicians filling out incident reports laid the blame on another individual in

---

28   Reason, J. "Human Error: Models and Management." *Bmj* 320, no. 7237 (2000): 768–770.

45 percent of the cases, while in 36 percent of the cases, the person actually logging the incident report blamed another individual as well.[29]

Only 2 percent of the health care providers reporting the incidents accepted the blame on themselves and took full responsibility.

Again, blaming others is easier than taking ownership of the situation. However, the UK researchers believe that successful improvements in health care is unlikely without getting to a blame-free culture![30] The study concluded that blame blinds us to "the contribution of system factors in others' behavior" and hinders us from identifying areas for improvement.[31]

Essentially, with blame, we jump over the "finding solutions" part of patient safety and try to label an incident with a particular person or name. In many cases, as we'll see in the following chapters, other factors can lead to a medical error, and as patients, we cannot afford to keep the Blame Game going on any longer.

---

29 Cooper, Jennifer, Adrian Edwards, Huw Williams, Aziz Sheikh, Gareth Parry, Peter Hibbert, Amy Butlin, Liam Donaldson, and Andrew Carson-Stevens. "Nature of Blame in Patient Safety Incident Reports: Mixed Methods Analysis of a National Database." *The Annals of Family Medicine* 15, no. 5 (2017): 455–61.

30 Ibid.

31 Ibid.

We don't have the extra time or energy to skip the "finding solutions" step.

If you're making it your purpose to improve the system, be part of the solution to end the cycle of blame because it only keeps us from making productive improvements.

CHAPTER 4:

WHEN TRAGEDY STRIKES

Imagine being put to sleep under the knife in the operating room and suddenly waking up just as your surgery has started. This is what happened to Donna Penner, a patient in Manitoba. She is still recovering from the traumatic experience—all because of an anesthesiology error that could have been prevented.

In 2008, Donna had unbearable abdominal pain, so she and her husband Brian set out to their local emergency room. When the doctor examined her, she was told she needed a laparoscopy at another clinic, which is a procedure to take a better look at internal organs, so she got to the O.R., ready for the exploratory surgery.

In an interview for the Canadian Patient Safety Institute (CPSI), Donna says, "I was told, 'Oh, you are going to be just fine. We are going to take very good care of you,' and those words came back to haunt me."[32]

On the day of the surgery, she felt herself drift off to sleep as the anesthesia kicked in, and, "The next thing I remember is waking up. I could still hear the O.R. staff making noise and doing work, and I thought, *Oh, good, the surgery over; I'm ok,*" Donna explains.[33]

The next chilling words Donna heard was, "Scalpel please," and she realized the surgery was far from over; it was just beginning.

"I could hear my heart on the monitor, and it kept going faster and faster and faster," recalling that her heartbeat reached the point where the doctor noticed that she was in distress and called for the anesthesiologist, but she remembers the nurses noting that **he wasn't there.**[34]

The Canadian Anesthesiologists' Society, a not-for-profit organization representing over three thousand Canadian

---

32 "Anesthesia Awareness Incident Makes Surgery A Nightmare Experience." Canadian Patient Safety Institute. 2016.

33 Ibid.

34 Ibid.

health practitioners, explains that anesthesiologists need to stay on-site in the O.R. to monitor the patient's heart rate and signs of distress.[35] So where was Donna's anesthesiologist during her surgery, because he certainly wasn't in the operation room where Donna needed him to be.

Donna's nightmare had just begun as she felt the surgeon make the first incision. "I wanted to scream at him to stop hurting me, but I quickly realized **I was paralyzed**."[36] She could feel the instruments in her abdomen and organs being shifted around. The anesthesiologist was suddenly back in the room and put something in her IV. "I don't know what it was, but it didn't make me go back to sleep," Donna explains.[37]

"I thought I was going to die...the pain was so horrific, I don't have the words to describe how much it hurt."[38]

— DONNA PENNER

Not being able to verbally speak, Donna was screaming in her head, pleading for everything to stop until she decided to mentally note her goodbyes to her family. "I thought about

---

35 Canadian Anesthesiologists' Society. "Anesthesia FAQ." 2019.
36 "Anesthesia Awareness Incident Makes Surgery A Nightmare Experience." Canadian Patient Safety Institute. 2016.
37 Ibid.
38 Ibid.

Brian and I thought about our children," Donna shares,[39] and you could see the pain in her eyes in the interview.

Although the surgery eventually ended, the nightmare was still not over for Donna. The first words out of her mouth as soon as she could speak were, "I was awake. I felt him cut me."[40]

There were only two nurses in the room, as well as the anesthesiologist at this time, and being in visible shock, **they just kept quiet.**

So Donna called for Brian.

Brian joined her in the recovery room, and they spoke with the anesthesiologist. He didn't say a word to Donna as she explained what had happened to her.

"And after I finished," she says in the interview with a quiver, "he simply shrugged his shoulders and he said, **'It happens sometimes.'** And he turned and walked out of my room."[41]

They spoke with the surgeon after that. Once he heard Donna's story, "He grabbed my hand with both of his hands and

---

39 Ibid.
40 Ibid
41 Ibid

he had tears in his eyes, and he said, 'I am so sorry this happened to you,'" Donna describes.

This whirlwind experience came and went while Donna and Brian were trying to grasp what had just happened. Hearing her story made me wonder what Donna's next steps were because, surely, she had questions that needed to be answered, the first being why the anesthesiologist wasn't in the O.R. to begin with.

DONNA'S NEXT STEPS

How does one handle a life event as traumatic as the one Donna experienced? From my conversation with her, it seems it takes strong people to do what Donna did.

I had reached out and had the honor of speaking with Donna a little while after I heard her story because I was invested in learning about her next steps after the medical error and how she was doing.

Who did she contact? What did she do? How does she play a role in patient safety initiatives now? How has her life changed after all these years since the medical error?

Donna mentioned that one of her most pressing questions was why the anesthesiologist wasn't in the room when she was under general anesthesia, as protocol dictated, but she wasn't getting the answers she was looking for. The anesthesiologist was not cooperating with Donna and her husband to explain what happened after that brief encounter she had with him on the day of her surgery. He and his team of lawyers and hospital staff were keeping completely quiet about the whole situation because of legal protocol, or so the hospital thought that was the way to go.

A little while into my research about patient safety, I came across "The Apology Act," which came into play in a few provinces and territories in Canada in 2009, including Manitoba in 2007, and it allows physicians and other health care providers to apologize without taking on the legal liabilities of the mistakes.[42] The act humanizes situations like Donna's and makes room for some sympathy where sympathy is due without the fear of legal burdens.

Apologies and accountability go a long way when we are wronged by someone else. We find closure in the mere words "I'm sorry." While apologies do not take away the hurt, they help us take one small step toward better mental health.

From reading many physician stories about their medical errors, one of the biggest reasons it took them longer to

---

42   "Apology Act, 2009, S.O. 2009, c. 3." Ontario: Search Laws. 2009.

speak out about their mistakes was fear. There is an insurmountable stigma around making medical errors, and while it makes sense for errors to be frowned upon, physicians often hesitate to go out of their way to offer emotional or mental support for patients because they fear the legal and financial liabilities.

The Apology Act encourages ownership on the physician's side and allows for dialogue between the patient and health care provider.

So I asked Donna why this Act didn't take effect when she demanded answers. Unfortunately, the Act was so new at that time and Donna believes the hospital wasn't familiar enough with the Act to use it to help her. Instead, they took a more protective stance and decided to say nothing rather than to put the hospital and the people involved in jeopardy.

It's frustrating to me how things can get so out of your control so fast, and in Donna's case, it was all due to legal protection from the hospital's side. She wasn't getting answers from the anesthesiologist, so she and her husband tried other ways to reach out to the people responsible.

After I asked Donna what anyone can do in that situation, she immediately said:

One of the first steps is go to the people responsible for all those different things. Try the doctor, or the nurse or the person responsible for the harm. If that person doesn't talk, **go higher, go higher**, keep going higher until you reach the top, like a VP medical service, the CEO, board members, the board chair.

By nature, Donna and Brian didn't want to take things to a more confrontational level, but in hindsight, she said they should have gone straight to the media.

"We thought we would take a gentle, assertive approach, and try to work with them and get them to see the damage that this has done. And for many years, I felt that that was the way for us to go," Donna explained.

There are so many resources to reach out to. As mentioned, the beauty of this health care system is it's so intricate, with many layers of staff. It's so important to not only take matters into your own hands but to try to break through the protective barriers that hospitals may put up.

While, in theory, this is all simple, it's one of the hardest journeys anyone can experience. It took Donna **six years** to get the anesthesiologist to talk to her, after years of asking and years of being told "no". When the anesthesiologist finally agreed to speak, Donna asked him the questions that had been left unanswered for years, "Why did you leave? What was so important that you had to leave me in the O.R. unattended, while under general anesthetic? Why did you go?"

His reply? **"I don't remember."**

I'm not trying to give health care providers and hospital staff a bad rep—they are the backbone of why and how we're getting most of our health needs met. I have so much respect for nurses, doctors, and anyone else who runs around in hospitals attending to patients because that sh*t's hard. One of the dangerous reasons for misconceptions about the health care system is generalizations, so take this as a moment to recognize Donna's situation as more of that individual anesthesiologist's mistake and not something that *all* anesthesiologists do.

However, this anesthesiologist not only took six years to talk to her, but when he did talk, he didn't give her the closure she had been searching for—now what?

Before this traumatic experience, Donna was a very active person and a real practical joker. In my interview with her, she explained that she used to be a very social employee and enjoyed working with others—I can personally relate to that, and I realized how easy it is to take the little things for granted.

Since the surgery in 2008, she was diagnosed with PTSD and life is very different for her. She had to leave her job and now experiences a great deal of memory and concentration issues. In the Canadian Patient Safety Institute interview, her husband explained that he never knows what each day will be like for her. It can be quite an emotional rollercoaster. One flashback can bring an onset of emotions and then "two hours later, the grandkids come over and it's a ray of sunshine again."[43]

She explained to me in our chat:

> I look outside in the morning, I get up and I see all these people hurrying off to work and I say to my husband, 'I'm so jealous' because I can't do that. I say to him, 'You come home from work and you've got funny stories to share with me; 'This happened at work and this person said this, and we laughed and laughed' or you have the little pranks you play on a coworker, or your boss gives you a compliment. You know those little things that build your self-esteem, that builds your confidence in yourself—**I miss that. I really, really miss that.**

***

---

43 "Anesthesia Awareness Incident Makes Surgery A Nightmare Experience." Canadian Patient Safety Institute. 2016.

However, even with all of this emotional turbulence going on, Donna is a superstar and should be an inspiration to all of us.

She said that while the anesthesiologist didn't cooperate with her, she was involved with a couple of projects because she wanted to share her story to make a dent in anesthesiology awareness. She worked with the region's patient safety guidelines for a little while and after years of asking, she was given the green light to create a patient group that had a voice to guideline the changes in the works.

Around a year after the medical error occurred, she also wanted to reach out to resident students hoping to open their eyes to the reality of their practice. She reached out to the University of Manitoba by simply "playing with Mr. Google one day," she explained to me.

Donna literally went to the University of Manitoba's website and searched for the Anesthesiology Department, where she found hundreds of names. She describes:

> I saw all these names on the screen and went, 'Oh my 'goodness,' so I went straight to the top and I checked out the department head and anesthesiologist, Dr. Eric Jacobsohn. Within minutes, I explained to him in an email what happened to me and that I was looking to spread the word among students.

Dr. Jacobsohn contacted her a little while later, and after speaking for several hours over the phone, he welcomed Donna to speak with his resident students, and they became great friends for years to come. This then opened another door of opportunity for Donna, where Dr. Jacobsohn invited her to speak at the University of Ottawa, alongside her husband, to resident students there. After her talk to a big audience, Donna recalls, "Dr. Jacobsohn turned to me, and he says, 'Are you ready for the next one?'" They flew to McGill University in Montreal, Quebec to speak with the anesthesia department there, and then to Whistler, British Columbia, and now recently, to an international conference for Anesthesiologists held in California.

Donna's been contacted for several phone interviews from the UK. Her story even made it all the way out to Mexico radio shows. About her entire journey, Donna said, "I didn't know what to do with all of this. But I [knew I needed] to turn this horrible, horrible experience into something better"—and she's done just that.

It's so easy for anyone to have given up and turned bitter after a gruesome journey like that, but Donna kept her head up and her heart open. From my research, this continuous, subtle optimism keeps patients determined after a serious medical error. In fact, open hearts might just be the key to recognize opportunities to help other people, meet amazing supports, and be a ray of inspiration for so many others.

Donna explained how there would be students in tears or patients reaching out to her about her story, and everyone was completely in awe of the effects of anesthesia awareness.

Although it's been years since the medical error, participating in talks is still difficult for Donna, and it does not get better with each talk she presents. But Donna told me she chooses to keep going even after all that, which is more rewarding than trying to get answers from people who don't want to cooperate.

Donna's story teaches us so many things, but the most important of all is there is no one *right* way of doing things. She is non-confrontational by nature and still managed to touch the hearts of thousands of people, two of them being you and I. Donna said nurses and students told her that the way they approach patients will be forever changed because of her talk—imagine having that influence.

***

According to the Canadian Anesthesiologists' Society, approximately one in one thousand general anesthetic practices lead to patient anesthesia awareness,[44] and with 37 million people in Canada, that's a lot of patients waking up in their surgeries.

I am not here to list all the things that went wrong with the system and with Donna's anesthesiology routine. For reasons still unclear even to her, the anesthesiologist who was supposed to be in the room with Donna wasn't there. Period.

My aim here is to applaud Donna for her courage and strength, not just through the medical error that she so heroically endured and survived, but the awareness she's raised on the matter as a whole. We should all look up to people like Donna because she certainly has made a dent in how anesthesia awareness is seen.

Donna showed us a way to *work with the system* rather than against it. If all you're getting is ignorance, give them silence and do your own thing. Donna has experienced silence from communities that should have supported her after her medical error, so instead, she decided to back off and take on better offers that educated future anesthesiologists and health care providers.

44　"What Is Anesthesia Awareness?". Canadian Anesthesiologists' Society. 2019.

Take a breather from your current situation, train your mind to slow down, reflect, and then pick the smartest move that will get you a bigger outcome. If a smarter move is avoiding a lawsuit that will only take years and energy off your life, and instead, going to the media and raising awareness is the best option, then, by all means, do it. You don't have to fight the system; you just have to help them improve, and Donna did that.

Donna found a way to be part of the solution instead of burning bridges and living by the misconception that everyone in health care is one big, ignorant monster. She built stepping-stones with what she had to work with and jumped to the next and the next until her voice grew a heck of a lot louder than having focused on the negative.

CHAPTER 5:

GRIEF

———

"There's always failure. And there's always disappointment. And there's always loss. But the secret is learning from the loss and realizing that none of those holes are vacuums"

— MICHAEL J. FOX

Grief comes in so many different forms and intensities that, while it may have a single dictionary definition, is a unique experience for everyone.

The first dictionary definition you'll find for grief is, "Deep and poignant distress caused by or as if by bereavement."[45] In

———

45 *Merriam-Webster*, s.v. "grief".

other words, the dictionary says that grief is anguish caused by the loss of someone or something in one's life.

That's true, but not quite.

The Grief Recovery Institute, an organization that offers one-on-one or group support for grievers in North America and Europe, has a different definition of grief—one that's clear and instantly hits home. To them, "Grief is the conflicting **feelings** caused by the end of, or change in, a familiar pattern of behavior."[46]

Their use of the word "feelings" makes this definition more accessible to all of us because grief can be a lot more than just "anguish" or "distress."

People can grieve over anything: the loss of a loved one, the loss of a life dream or big job opportunity, the loss of financial stability, the loss of a sense of safety, the loss of a lifestyle, and even the loss of one's prior state of health.

These losses can bring us sadness, hopelessness, confusion, anger, frustration, trauma, numbness, and the list goes on and on. When I interviewed medical error survivors, I couldn't stop thinking about the emotional journey they

---

46 Friedman, Russell. "The Best Grief Definition You Will Find". *The Grief Recovery Method*. 2013.

must have walked through, and I imagined the process being very similar to the way someone grieves over a loss of any kind.

Grief does not have to just be associated with the death of a loved one, and it's important to understand why you feel the things you feel after a medical error.

One reason I'm interested in the way grief works is that, a few years ago, I noticed that for a good portion of my life, I'd been grieving the death of two people I barely got to know growing up.

My parents and I moved to Canada when I was four, and one of the earliest memories I have is of my first day of kindergarten. At that time, my parents were the first of their families to move out of our home country and start a new life from scratch.

Once in Canada, we would keep in touch with our family back home and I'd regularly talk to my aunts, uncles, and grandparents. I only knew what they looked like through photographs, so I'd use the pictures to match faces with voices.

This was way before the age of Face Time since technology had just come so far as making flip phones and those boxy desktop computers.

A few years later, though I can't recall ever processing the news, my grandmother on my dad's side passed away. I got to know her just through stories and pictures, but had she been alive today, I know my grandma and I would have been really close.

In 2007, we took a family trip to our home country to visit family, and although I never met my grandma because of her passing, I met the rest of my grandparents. I got to know my grandpa on my dad's side well during my time there.

Years after my month-long time with him, my grandpa passed away in a tragic car accident. I remember the news of his passing quite clearly, and I was old enough to understand how hard it was for my parents. Even then, though, I don't remember crying or "grieving" heavily over his death, since I didn't have the close connection with him (or at least enough connection to feel the loss). I just recall trying to act courteously during our own little gathering in Canada for his passing, steering clear of my dad as he coped with his loss, and seeing life get back to normal a little while later.

As a child, my grandparents' deaths weren't life-changing events for me. I just didn't understand it, so I guess I wasn't affected by their losses at all—I don't think I even shed a single tear in the years surrounding their deaths.

Interestingly, when I was around nineteen, I had a sudden need to learn more about my grandparents and what they were like. I had a vague idea of what grandpa was like, but not so much of my nana. But the more I learned about them, like how my nana's laugh was contagious or how my grandpa loved my sister and I so unconditionally, I would get more and more emotional.

In fact, in 2018, while I was a writer for HerCampus, I devoted an article in the form of a letter just for them, later on deciding not to publish it for the public. That year, to my surprise, I ended up shedding many tears for my grandparents. I badly wanted them to have been alive all these years to see me grow and be accomplished.

These are some excerpts from the article I wrote but never published:

***

"To the grandma I never got to know:

At age 9, I never understood how much my life would change without you here because, to be frank, how can you miss someone you don't remember meeting? A few years after your passing, I found out about grandpa passing too and became more aware of the meaning of losing a loved one, even if I hadn't known him all that much either.

But for reasons I can't explain, even if the last time I met you was when I wasn't old enough to remember, I'm missing you a little extra now. But it's baffling because again…how do you miss someone who you don't remember meeting?

Grandpa,

I don't know where to begin, but I just want to thank you for your presence in my life, albeit very short. I wish I was able to know more about you and how much of a wonderful grandfather you were.

I will always keep your kindness in my heart, and I will always look up to you. I heard you had a big heart, and I try to pass that on from you. I know you both loved me so much, and I hope you know how much I love you too."

***

I spoke to a friend about how I felt because I didn't know how to process these feelings and tears, especially mid-exam season when I was already walking on emotional thin ice because of the usual school stresses.

She summed it up so perfectly. She said, "Maybe you're not actually grieving your own personal relationship with them, but instead, you're grieving their *absence* in your life?"

Mind. Freaking. Blown.

Maybe...I was grieving **what could have been**.

So while their death hadn't phased me for a while, their empty "placemats" grew to be bigger and bigger voids in my life as I got to create personas for them in my mind.

People can grieve for the strangest reasons, and sometimes, depending on other life circumstances, we may suddenly start grieving something that in the years past we were *okay* with. When I even *attempt* to identify with those who have experienced a medical error, I imagine that not only would I be grieving the health or person I lost, I'd also bitterly grieve what *could have been* had the medical error *not* happened.

COULD HAVES

"Grieving is about loss, not just death"

— STIGMA FIGHTERS

A lot of studies structured around grief relating to the loss of loved ones discuss a general process that the grieving go through:[47]

1. Numbness
2. Emotional trauma from the distress of separation
3. Mourning and despair
4. Eventual recovery or reorganization.

While studies on grief look at the literal loss of a loved one, you can also grieve the loss of a lifestyle you once had, whether it's a physical ability you no longer have due to a medical error or an alteration in your life that makes you reminisce about life before the medical harm—i.e., what could have been if the error hadn't occurred.

Wherever you are on this vast spectrum of medical harm, accepting your present circumstance and going from despair to eventual recovery can be one of the hardest hurdles to get over; in fact, people sometimes stay in the phase of despair forever.

It is only understandable to go through different layers of emotions, at times even conflicting ones. I see the grief of

---

47   PDQ Board. 2017. "Grief, Bereavement, And Coping With Loss". National Cancer Institute (US).

medical error a little different from the grief we experience when a negative event occurs naturally and was foreseeable.

For instance, Abigail* was diagnosed with throat cancer later in her life but experienced a "could have" as well.

*Names and details have been changed for simplicity, but this story is based on the same concepts.

One day, Abigail sensed pain in her throat and went to her physician to get examined but was sent home, being told it was a common sore throat. She went in a second time because the pain didn't stop, but this time was given medication to only relieve her pain. After a grueling few months, Abigail went back yet again, but this time she insisted on an endoscopy procedure, which detects abnormal cells in tissue. The results came back, and Abigail had been diagnosed with an aggressive type of throat cancer that could have been caught early on.

She underwent chemotherapy treatment and the cancer never came back, but some patients go past the point of no return where treatment doesn't guarantee survival.

However, I couldn't help but think of a second, slightly bearable journey of cancer diagnosis that Abigail could have experienced instead.

She could have been sent to a specialist and undergone endoscopy a lot sooner. Period.

Regardless of how Abigail's journey panned out after this event—whether the cancer persisted or went away—her fate would have been more determined by the natural cycle of cancer rather than a medical error, because the cancer was detected as soon as possible.

With or without an early diagnosis, the entire journey of cancer and chemotherapy is physically, mentally, and emotionally demanding, but the addition of medical error makes things even more frustrating.

The two versions of Abigail's story are worlds apart. The more bearable scenario, being treated early on, is bearable because you're only dealing with an unfortunate, *natural* life event.

The late-diagnosis scenario that Abigail actually experienced *Could. Have. Been. Prevented.*

This whole notion of "could have" is the culprit behind the added levels of agony that medical error survivors may feel after they've experienced unfortunate medical errors that 'could have' not happened.

Abigail 'could have' been diagnosed earlier, because had that happened, she may have been saved from the stress of undergoing extensive chemo. Cal Sheridan's CT scan 'could have' been read thoroughly, because had his kernicterus development been caught, his cerebral palsy may have been a lot different now. Donna's anesthesiologist 'could have' been in the room while her body was showing signs of anesthesia awareness because had he realized it, she wouldn't have undergone such horrendous trauma.

These "could haves" only bring about more pain because they bring up a world of better outcomes had the medical errors not happened, so besides grieving what you've lost, you're also grieving about what could have happened.

It's important to recognize the differences in the two types of griefs because they can be easily left unacknowledged. Understanding exactly what type of grief you are experiencing is so crucial for your mind and soul. Reflecting on specifically *where* and *why* those emotions around your grief are coming from can help find some clarity and make powerful steps in patient safety.

CHAPTER 6:

FORGIVENESS

——

In his article for The Guardian, Daniel Poskitt recalls the tragic day he found out that his sister, Karen, was stabbed to death by her boyfriend, who subsequently faced fifteen years in prison.[48] Daniel was seventeen at the time and the numbness and sorrow he felt years after were near suffocating, mainly because there were so many unanswered questions.

This is a true story I stumbled upon while trying to understand the nature of forgiveness.

Ten years passed and Daniel said in an interview to "The Guardian" that he had slowly sorted out his life and adjusted to the absence of his sister, but his family's peace was yet

48 "I Was Able To Forgive My Sister's Murderer Only By Acknowledging My Own Anger". The Guardian. 2015.

again disrupted by an offer from the prison to meet with the killer to get some closure. After deliberation, the family accepted the offer and the day came to actually meet him.

The family walked into a room with just a circle of chairs, and once they were seated, the offender walked in. Daniel recalls not being prepared for such a sudden confrontation, especially being in such close proximity to him.

After years of sorrow, the family finally had the chance to ask the boyfriend his reason for killing Karen—and the offender said he didn't know why. The day she died was so long ago according to him, that he "couldn't remember the details."[49]

"For our family, this was unacceptable – we had come for answers," Daniel explained...and yet they got nothing answered.[50]

That day, Daniel had hoped to get all the answers he needed to rest easy—he was literally staring into the eyes of the only person in the world who had the answers—and even then, he still didn't get his closure.

---

49 Ibid.
50 Ibid.

Daniel understood that he had to put his sister's death in the past, regardless of how torturous the offender was being. His family still didn't have answers, but at that very moment, Daniel decided that he would move on. He said in the interview:

> That may sound strange to some people, but I've learnt that forgiveness is not about the perpetrator, **it's about you**. It's about you letting go of the stuff that holds you back so you can live a happy and fulfilling life.[51]

I agree with Daniel—forgiveness *is* all about you. It's about your own closure and mental clarity. Forgiveness can look different for everyone, and the path to achieve it varies. For Daniel, when he was sitting face to face with his sister's killer and could not get a word from him about what had happened the day she died, all he could muster up the strength to do was to yell, "You fucking coward" at his face.[52]

While I am by no means condoning going up to everyone who wrongs us and yelling in their faces, Daniel showed that sometimes the time and energy we spend on finding answers may seem worth the while, but if the agony of wanting to

---

51 "I Was Able To Forgive My Sister's Murderer Only By Acknowledging My Own Anger". The Guardian. 2015.
52 Ibid.

know "why" is making us take steps back instead of forward, it might be time to reevaluate.

THE SECOND VICTIM

Patients who experience harm in medical settings have no doubt been victimized by preventable mistakes, but the second victim refers to health care providers who make the medical errors directly. Whether they are the sources of the errors or are part of the many other factors that cause them, many health care providers who have made medical errors face their own traumas. To some, it may sound borderline offensive to say that health care providers are also "victims" when they cause harm, but the reality is just that.

My goal for you, as someone who was *directly* harmed during a medical error, is to gain a complete understanding of what goes into medical errors so you can use this information to your benefit rather than resentment.

Knowing how intricate and flawed the system is will show you where to place your focus if you are seeking confrontation or legal action. Compassion may not be what you are seeking if you're left angry from the medical error, this is understandable—but it is essential to gain a good understanding of both sides to the story.

Health care providers experience tremendous guilt, fear, emotional pain, and sometimes even shame—understanding this whole other side of medical error can open doors of clarity for medical error survivors.

To process the fact that someone's life ended, or they were close to death, because of *your* actions and *your* calls can be traumatizing beyond belief. We need to reflect on why health care providers have such a difficult time fessing up to their mistakes and help create an environment where opening up to errors is encouraged.

While we shouldn't downplay that health care providers shouldn't be making the mistakes in the first place, in reality, they are for now.

The second victim was first introduced into Public Health in a paper published in 2000 by Albert Wu called, "Medical error: the second victim."[53] In this paper, Wu explains the importance of coming clean to the families of the patient and colleagues once a mistake is made, but clarifies that often, the opportunity to talk about mistakes is simply not there. While many changes have been made to the health care system and its policies since 2000, the suggestions in Wu's paper can still

---

53 Wu, Albert. "Medical Error: The Second Victim". *BMJ* 320 (2000): 726-727.

be applied today when health care providers face difficulties of 'coming clean.'

As Wu says:

> It has been suggested that the only way to face the guilt after a serious error is through confession, restitution, and absolution. But confession is discouraged, passively by the lack of...forums for discussion, and sometimes actively by risk managers and hospital lawyers.[54]

In my interviews, I've often been reminded that health care providers don't go into work thinking they will harm someone that day. While their intentions may be patient-centered, unfortunately, sometimes their actions or the system do not align with that notion.

Health care providers do make mistakes due to their own slip-ups, which many patients understandably believe should not happen in the first place. In the following sections, you will hear from health care providers who have made fatal or near-fatal mistakes in their practice. Their side of the story gave me a completely new lens for the health care system that goes beyond the doctors and nurses we interact with.

---

54 Ibid.

***

"To err is human, to forgive is divine"

— ALEXANDER POPE, AN EIGHTEENTH-CENTURY
ENGLISH POET IN *AN ESSAY ON CRITICISM.*

This famous quote in the world of patient safety refers to the idea that it is human nature to make mistakes but *divine* nature to forgive others because forgiveness is harder. So if, as humans, we aren't made perfect, does it not make sense to focus our attention on how the system is built rather than trying to perfect whoever is working the front-line?

I was surprised to learn that our system often sets up health care providers for failure: Medication mislabeling, short staff, long hours, messy environment, compensation—or lack thereof in some cases—miscommunication between health care branching systems, and the list continues.

The International Society for Quality in Health Care (ISQua) is a non-profit, global organization that has built a community aimed to promote universal high-quality health care. The president of ISQua and Australian professor in health systems research, Dr. Jeffrey Braithwaite, published a paper called, "Changing how we think about health care improvement."

In his article, he writes:

> We focus on the 10 percent of adverse events while
> mostly overlooking the 90 percent of care that has no
> harm...If we better appreciate how clinicians handle
> dynamic situations throughout the day, constantly
> adapting, and getting so much right, we can begin
> to identify the factors that underpin that success.[55]

I imagined Dr. Braithwaite's words as an analogy. Consider
this: The health care system itself is the ice that health care
providers skate on, from one patient to the other. If the ice is
thin, isn't it only a matter of time before it cracks and breaks?
Sometimes health care staff are given only so much foundation to work with, and one of our roles as patients can be to
help strengthen the ice. We can use our experiences to speak
up to medication manufacturers, policymakers, governments,
hospital boards of directors, medical students, ministries of
health, etc. to get our message across.

***

Remembering Donna Penner's story, while we can't be sure
why Donna's nurses and anesthesiologist kept quiet as she
was desperate for an explanation post-surgery, I can be sure

55 Braithwaite, Jeffrey. "Changing How We Think About Healthcare
    Improvement". *BMJ* 361 (2018).

of one thing—Donna needed a listening ear at the time of her crisis and was not given one until later when the surgeon spoke with her. In Donna's CPSI interview, she explains, "Even if it's only 'I'm so sorry,' that means so much to the patient that has been traumatized or harmed in health care."[56] Donna isn't the only one who believes in the power, and skill, of apology.

Dr. Amy Nakajima, an obstetrician and gynecologist working alongside the University of Ottawa's Faculty of Medicine, recalls a nightmare experience she had back in 2001. She says in a CPSI interview that she thought about the experience daily for the first ten years after the medical chaos had occurred. "It never left me," she explains, somber.[57]

In 2001, just fourteen months into her practice as an obstetrician-gynecologist, Dr. Nakajima was called in to help tend to a woman in labor. The newborn baby's heart rate was dipping, so it was protocol to get a second opinion from a physician. Newborns' heartbeats can sometimes dip and then accelerate back to the expected heartbeat, but routinely, it should always be monitored. So, per usual, Dr. Nakajima took over the vacuum delivery, an assisted-birth technique that the family

---

56 "Anesthesia Awareness Incident Makes Surgery A Nightmare Experience." Canadian Patient Safety Institute. 2016.
57 "Patient's Unexpected Death Changes The Way One Obstetrician Thinks All Doctors Should Be Educated." Canadian Patient Safety Institute. 2016.

doctor already initiated. Everything was going as expected and the delivery went smoothly.

After giving birth, Dr. Nakajima noticed the mother had a vaginal tear, so she was taken to the operating room for Dr. Nakajima to take a closer look for a repair. She and her team expected the bleeding to stop after the standard repair routine, but it didn't. There is a usual algorithm for women who bleed after delivery, but after a few procedures, this mother's bleeding still didn't stop. The anesthesiologist on duty also wasn't getting the expected results that came with his usual anesthesiology procedures, so Dr. Nakajima and the anesthesiologist called their second on-calls for extra help.

Even with the added assistance, the team was clearly still struggling, so now a general surgeon was called. Then it started drifting into, "This doesn't feel right; This isn't working; She's not responding in the way I'm expecting her to respond; **We're all struggling now,**" Dr. Nakajima recalls grimly.[58]

The team had done everything they could and exhausted all of their options, but they brought the mother to ICU, where she ultimately passed away.

---

58 Ibid.

This incident turned what should have been a beautiful day for a mother welcoming her newborn into the world to a nightmare that took the life of a mother who didn't get to carry her baby home—and a whole different nightmare for Dr. Nakajima as a practicing health care provider.

She recalls somber:

How was I supposed to talk to the patient's family? What was I supposed to say? I had not been coached in my residency program. I never watched a [health care] provider have an event like this and to talk to the family afterwards? To provide information; to provide emotional support to the family; and to also figure out what happened? For all those reasons, I felt inept because I hadn't been trained [how to handle this grim situation].[59]

After a sleepless night of reviewing protocols, dictations, and notes from that delivery, Dr. Nakajima realized that the patient probably didn't need a few procedures she had undergone while induced, "and it became a very acute, painful unscheduled teaching for me about how to do an incision analysis. And yet nobody told me how to do this."[60]

---

59 "Patient's Unexpected Death Changes The Way One Obstetrician Thinks All Doctors Should Be Educated." Canadian Patient Safety Institute. 2016.
60 Ibid.

The autopsy results came a little while later, and revealed the mother had experienced a rare event that caused a blockage in a blood vessel—even so, Dr. Nakajima said she was not prepared for that to ever happen.

Therein lies the power of ownership. Dr. Nakajima faced the nightmare of losing a patient by taking it upon herself to articulate to the family what happened and be there for them as a source of emotional support. She attended the mother's funeral and explains, "I don't think I'll ever forget that. [Many people attended] and it was completely full. I felt so sorry for this family."[61]

"It really inspired me to advocate for more patient safety teaching in undergraduate and postgraduate education," and she has worked closely with the Faculty of Medicine at the University of Ottawa.[62]

Dr. Nakajima explains that the way providers break bad news to a family can be so fundamentally different. "I can say, 'I'm really sorry, remember the tests that we did last time? It shows that you have cervical cancer.'" Dr. Nakajima puts things in a great perspective. She says that, yes, having cervical cancer is terrible news for a patient, and health care

---

61 Ibid.
62 Ibid.

providers will feel terrible giving that news to the patient because they know what's coming. "But that's fundamentally different from [you] saying, 'I'm really sorry; you have breast cancer. We removed the wrong breast.'"[63]

It was eye-opening to me that Dr. Nakajima took full ownership and spread the word about her mistakes. With Dr. Nakajima's work, other health care providers can keep the rare event the mother experienced in mind when administering surgeries—but what if the system doesn't always encourage health care providers to speak up?

---

63 Ibid.

CHAPTER 7:

THE OTHER SIDE

——

Danielle Ofri, a practicing internist in New York City's Bellevue Hospital, presented a TEDMED talk about the chilling error she made so early into the start of her hospital placement.

"Four months into my internship, I nearly killed a patient and I didn't tell a soul," Dr. Ofri explains.[64]

Danielle was working during a particularly busy hospital season in New York City. "Our patients were dreadfully, brutally sick," Danielle explains.[65] One quiet, elderly patient in particular was assessed to have an altered mental status, but

---

64 Danielle Ofri,. "Deconstructing Our Perception of Perfectionism." 2015. TEDMED video.
65 Ibid.

doctors believed it was because of his "touch of dementia," as Danielle described. She recalls that his lab tests were read aloud to her and the radiology results were said to be "fine"—he was assessed as totally stable.

Stable patients are usually transferred to another wing reserved for patients waiting to be discharged, so Danielle decided this elderly man was ready to be discharged as well—his tests were said to be "all clear."

"It wasn't until the next morning I learned that my 'totally stable patient' actually had an intracranial hemorrhage—he was bleeding into his brain," Danielle explains.[66] It was then clear to Danielle that his altered mental status wasn't completely due to his dementia.

When the radiology results were read out loud to her as, "Radiology: fine" by someone else, Danielle didn't look at the scan herself. She missed the computerized tomography scan (CT scan) that would have clearly shown that her patient had a brain hemorrhage and instead, she sent him to the discharge wing.

---

66 Ibid.

By *sheer luck*, a radiology resident had reassessed the scan that night and gotten the patient the help he needed to stay alive and survive the near-miss medical error.

"I was horrified at myself for not having done due diligence for my patient. I was so ashamed that I didn't tell anyone—not that day, not for twenty-five years," Danielle explains as the TEDMED room became chillingly silent.[67]

Danielle's brush with patient death brought her so much shame, guilt, and fear that she ended up dealing with for years afterward.

By seeing other professionals get a talk-down from her Chief of Surgery for other mistakes in the past, the message Danielle had perceived as a young practitioner was, "Anything short of perfection is failure," she explains.[68]

Danielle was so afraid to say anything about her first near-miss encounter that the error remained forever hidden, uncounted, unstudied, *unremedied* until she spoke up.

While every medical error is different and each health care provider even more so, it's important to acknowledge the

---

67 Ibid.
68 Danielle Ofri, "Deconstructing Our Perception of Perfectionism." 2015. TEDMED video.

message about impossible expectations many health care providers are getting from their superiors, like Danielle's Chief of Surgery, for instance.

Danielle's mistake shouldn't be justified, because, yes, she should have read the scan herself. But no matter how many times we say, "Danielle shouldn't have made that mistake," her medical error won't disappear.

As a health care provider, the next best step to take after an encounter like Danielle's is accepting the mistake, speaking up, and warning others in the field to beware of the same errors. Some doctors *are* standing up to gaps in the system, like Danielle, among other health care practitioners and researchers…but others are still not.

Danielle has written blogs on the blunt health care issues America faces, along with political policies that put patients and physicians in harm to raise more awareness on medical error.

Herein lies the difference between productive and unproductive health care staff—what the individual practitioner does with their mistakes defines the fate of future patients and other practitioners.

It's our job to seek individuals who aren't afraid to speak up and challenge those who may be stuck in older mindsets that stigmatize mistakes and "imperfection" in practices.

We often hear of "practitioner burn out" in medicine. A study from the British Journal in 2008 tested for depression among residents in pediatrics.

Residents that experienced depression made six times as many medication errors each month than individuals who were not depressed.[69] The study also discussed the negative effects that depressed physicians can have on the quality of care that patients receive, so if our present system stigmatizes open discussions among practitioners, how will we take care of the people taking care of us?

Learning from each other is how humans thrive, and the more people speak up, the more statistics we have to create safer hospitals and medical settings for both patients and health care providers.

It would be wonderful to live in a world where doctors made no mistakes, but in reality, they do. Instead of putting more

---

69 Fahrenkopf, Amy M, Theodore C Sectish, Laura K Barger, Paul J Sharek, Daniel Lewin, Vincent W Chiang, Sarah Edwards, Bernhard L Wiedermann, and Christopher P Landrigan. "Rates of Medication Errors among Depressed and Burnt out Residents." *Bmj* 336, no. 7642 (2008): 488–91.

pressure on our health care providers, we need to place more pressure on the system and whoever has the power to improve it—policymakers, politicians, hospital board of directors, pharmacies, and manufacturers, and that's just scraping the surface.

This is where the power of partnership comes into play. Partnering up with hospitals and big organizations like the World Health Organization, The Canadian Patient Safety Institute, and the United Nations is a surefire way to find a professional in-patient safety who wants to hear your medical error story and help you make a difference. All the while, you will be supporting the health care providers and researchers who want to make a difference in the system as well, and together, you can find a solution to your medical error.

***

I listened in a talk by Dr. Thomas Aloia, a hepatobiliary oncologist from the University of Texas. He was presenting at the 2016 American College of Surgeons National Surgical Quality Improvement Program (NSQIP) about the goal of 'Zero'—Zero infections, zero never-events, **zero harm.**

He mentioned the accuracy of the comparisons we make between hospital safety and commercial airlines. I've heard the argument that if airlines can assure flyers' safety, excluding the fifteen to twenty crashes a year, then hospitals can equally assure the safety of patients.

Dr. Aloia says otherwise. Pilots fly the same predictable, perfectly maintained planes, while surgeons operate on different people every day, bringing on a whole onset of unpredictability.[70]

"If you let me operate on JJ Watt and do the same operation every day, we'll get to zero."[71]

— DR. ALOIA

In other words, people are different, and our bodies are built in unique ways that can react differently to the same "routine" operations. A routine operation may not affect one person in the same way as someone else, and somewhere in the chaos, other factors are thrown around and some are dodged until a medical error occurs.

Going back to our idea of perfection yet again, it's not worth meditating and agonizing over having a zero-harm system in place. Instead, we need to focus our energy as patients on

---

70 Thomas Aloia, "Patient Safety: Should Zero be the Goal?". 2017. MD Anderson Cancer Center.

71 Ibid.

what we've experienced and what we want to happen differently next time.

***

In November 2007, Dennis Quaid, an American actor, experienced an event he only could describe as "the scariest, most frightening day that [my wife and I] have ever been through. To come face to face with your little kids, who are so young in that kind of situation."[72]

After years of trying to conceive, and after five miscarriages, Dennis and his wife, Kimberly, chose surrogacy, hoping to have kids. In 2007, they finally welcomed their twins, Thomas Boone and Zoe Grace, into their life and were dispatched from the hospital to start a new chapter. As any parent would be, Dennis said in an interview with Dr. Mehmet Oz and Oprah Winfrey, "[Kimberly and I] were so happy to be able to be blessed by those two...They both came out so perfect."[73]

Only days after the twins came home, they developed a staphylococcus infection, which usually affects the nose and skin.

---

72 Steve Kroft. "Dennis Quaid Recounts Twins' Drug Ordeal". *CBS News*. 2008.

73 "The Quaid Family's Medical Nightmare Video". *Oprah WInfrey Network*. 2009.

In newborns, staph infections can be life-threatening but can also be treated with antibiotics—the earlier the better.

The Quaids brought their twins to Cedars-Sinai, a non-profit hospital in Los Angeles per doctor recommendation for routine antibiotic treatment. They were told they could leave their twins at the hospital and go back home until they received a call to pick them up again. In an interview with Claudia Kalb in 2010, Dennis said he had given the hospital explicit instructions to be called in case anything went wrong.[74] At 9 p.m. that night, Kimberly experienced a sudden wave of panic. "I just had this horrible feeling come over me, and I felt like the babies were passing—I just had this feeling of dread," she explained.[75]

Kimberly had such a strong intuitive feeling that she even made a little note on her calendar of the exact time she felt the dread at home. Dennis then called the hospital right away to check on the twins, and was told they were "'just fine'…but they weren't," Dennis recalls.[76]

74 Claudia Kalb. "Dennis Quaid: Making Hospitals Safer". *Newsweek*. 2010.
75 "The Quaid Family's Medical Nightmare Video". *Oprah WInfrey Network*. 2009.
76 "The Quaid Family's Medical Nightmare Video". *Oprah WInfrey Network*. 2009.

It was later found out the twins were actually experiencing a life-threatening danger that very night, and the Quaids were not told at the time. Dennis had even called the hospital once more that night and the nurses told him everything was going well.

It was only until the next morning that the Quaids went to the hospital and were greeted by their pediatrician and the hospital's lawyers.

They found out that over an eight-hour period, instead of receiving Hep-Lock U/P, a blood-thinner for newborns to clear up their IV lines and prevent blood clots, the twins received two doses of Heparin, the adult version of Hep-Lock, which is one thousand times stronger.

"The ten units that our kids were supposed to get, they got ten thousand. What it did was it basically turned their blood to the consistency of water," Dennis explains.[77] While Dennis was in the room the next morning, the twins were bleeding uncontrollably, and one of them was bleeding out of his bellybutton. The doctors were trying to "clamp" his son's bellybutton closed, and he recalls blood spraying as far as six feet, hitting the wall.[78]

---

77 Ibid.
78 Ibid.

"It was avoidable. Completely avoidable," Dennis says about the medical error that almost caused his newborn twins to die.

Around the forty-one-hour mark, after the Quaids got to the hospital, the twins were recovering, and by twenty-one days, they came back home healthy. While the Quaid family had a happy ending, sadly, this mix-up in blood thinners has happened in the past, resulting in fatalities.

A study by Jason Arimura and the research team at Lucile Packard Children's Hospital at Stanford looked into neonatal Heparin overdose. Their study mentions that in September 2006, six premature infants experienced a similar event as the Quaid twins, with only three of the six babies surviving—and that was just during *one month* in 2006.[79]

Even though it can be tempting to blame the sole nurse responsible for administering the blood-thinner to the Quaid twins, dealing with a situation like this with resentment and anger may do more harm than good.

---

79 Arimura, Jason, Robert Poole, Michael Jeng, William Rhine, and Paul Sharek. "Neonatal Heparin Overdose—A Multidisciplinary Team Approach to Medication Error Prevention." *The Journal of Pediatric Pharmacology and Therapeutics* 13, no. 2 (2008): 96–98.

In the interview with Claudia, Dennis highlights the importance of working through the anger and pain to cooperate with the health care providers to create a brighter future for the next newborn baby who develops a staph infection.

Dennis told Claudia he "doesn't really know" what happened to the nurse who administered the drug. They did not keep in touch with the nurses through this nightmare of a hospital visit, but Dennis said he didn't blame them.

"They're overworked, under-appreciated. The reason they get into health care to begin with is they're there to ease human suffering and they really do care," Dennis advocates.[80]

In fact, Dennis decided not to file a lawsuit against the hospital but, instead, sued the company that sent out Heparin to the hospitals in the area.

For Dennis' case, months before his twins were administered the high dose of Heparin, the company Baxter that was sourcing hospitals with the adult and infant version of Heparin made a label-change in the vials of both drugs. This change further differentiated the vial colors and sizes of the two drugs to prevent further medication errors...but it turned

---

80 "The Quaid Family's Medical Nightmare Video". *Oprah WInfrey Network.* 2009.

out that the old batches weren't recalled. These old vials were administered to the Quaid twins.

"They recall toasters, they recall trucks, they even recall dog food, but they don't recall medicine that kills people if you give it in the wrong dosage?"

— DENNIS QUAID

Baxter's Senior Director, Debra Bello, responded to Dennis' case in the same interview and addressed why the drug manufacturing company didn't recall the old vials. Baxter believed the hospital's administration of the drug was the issue and not the old medication label, because the drug itself was safe—it was just the new coloring and sizes that were different.

"One of the most important components of medication administration is to read the label and not rely on color, shape, or size," Debra explains.[81] The nurse who medicated the Quaid twins was held responsible for the mix-up, and Baxter thought itself to have no fault in this situation.

Right away, blame is already going around, and with big corporations being supported by strong lawyers, sometimes

---

81   Ibid.

the blame game may never end. Sure, the nurse may have read the wrong label and ideally *shouldn't* have made the medication mistake, but there is more to the story than we hear from the media.

While it's valid that parents and patients feel pain, hurt, anger, resentment, frustration, and all the emotions that come with life-altering medical errors, Dennis Quaid used his indescribable emotions as fuel to help make a positive difference in the hospital's dynamic.

The Cedars-Sinai hospital has invested more than $100 million in more advanced technology since the Quaid twins' near misses. This new technology uses barcode scanners to dispense medication doses to ensure the prescribed drug matches the patient's medical history.

"The problem is that [this medical error] happens over thousands of hospitals in this country every day," Dennis explains.[82] Dennis' family could have gone down a gruesome lawsuit route, and the hospital could have not cooperated as much as it did with the Quaids; however, both sides came together and ensured that this mistake did not happen again.

A partnership played an important component once again.

---

82 "The Quaid Family's Medical Nightmare Video". *Oprah WInfrey Network*. 2009.

Dennis did one of the best things a patient could do in that situation—tackle the system and not the imperfect human being. The new system in place at Cedars-Sinai can more confidently ensure that fewer Heparin medication mix-ups will happen again in the future—and that's what matters most.

CHAPTER 8:

THE DOMINO EFFECT

———

Elizabeth Cady Stanton. Henry Gerber. Tarana Burke.

These three individuals started some of the biggest movements in history, showing how one person can make a difference in society.

In 1815, Elizabeth Cady Stanton was born into a wealthy family, her father being a slave owner. As a judge himself, he
pushed Elizabeth toward studying law, and through her studies, Elizabeth grew frustrated at all the unjust laws toward
women.

She continued her studies until college, where she was forced
to go straight into the workplace without getting her college

degree because, at that time, women weren't allowed to seek post-secondary education.

Over time, through mutual friends, Elizabeth met an abolitionist, Henry Stanton, and followed suit in supporting the Anti-Slavery Movement. In 1840, Elizabeth and Henry married, but Elizabeth, wanting to end old-fashioned traditions, insisted on taking out the word 'obey' in her wedding vows—talk about girl-power in the '1800s.

For their honeymoon, the couple went to London for the World Anti-Slavery delegation, but once they got there, to her dismay, the convention didn't allow women delegates to attend.

Elizabeth's frustrations about women's rights ignited exponentially because of this.

She consulted with four other women to create the first Women's Rights Convention—also known as the Seneca Falls Convention—to give women a chance to attend conferences. Elizabeth also presented the Declaration of Sentiments, which was a document she modeled after the Declaration of Independence, to outline the discrimination women were facing at that time and what women's rights should be instead.

Through this courageous act, Elizabeth became well-known for her activism and met with Susan B. Anthony—another strong female activist.

Together, the two women made an enormous dent in raising women's voices about unjust laws and societal expectations—and they got the ball rolling for women's freedom all around the world.

Elizabeth started what is now recognized as the Women's Rights Movement.[83]

***

In 1923, Henry Gerber of Germany had just finished his three-year tour of duty in World War I. After the war, there was a rise in support for the homosexual community in Germany. People were advocating for the safety and freedom of all homosexuals, and Henry was inspired. Henry returned to Chicago, where his family lived, and wanted to start a similar movement in America, but he was wildly disappointed.

He realized Americans at that time didn't have the strong support for homosexuals he thought, and homosexuality was

---

83 "The Women's Rights Movement, 1848-1920." United States House of Representatives. 2019.

strictly repressed in society. It took Henry a year to find just six supporters to get activism started.

Then in 1924, Henry and his six supporters founded the Society for Human Rights—America's first-known gay rights organization.

To get the news across the country, Henry started a newsletter called 'Friendship and Freedom' and was publishing articles on his Society's work. However, once the news spread, Henry was arrested and detained in prison for three days. He lost his job, and his and his Society's name was quickly erased from the public record.

But Henry didn't give up.

Knowing he couldn't keep writing with his name out in the open, Henry sent submissions to the editor of the newspaper under a different name—Parisex—and so his writing continued under his new author name. Henry published his next work called "In Defense of Homosexuality"," but because of the Society's disappearance from the public record, the public couldn't read his work.

In 1952, when a new group—Mattachine Society—started their own publication, "One," Henry wrote to them and told them about his previous efforts.

Eventually, all of his work from the Society for Human Rights was released to the public, and he continued his activism to make rights equal for all who identified as homosexual.

Henry is known as the founder of the first gay rights organization in the United States.[84]

***

In 1996, Tarana Burke was a youth camp director, predominantly for children of color. Part of her job was to offer a listening ear to any youth who needed it. So, through the youth camps, she heard many heartbreaking stories from kids who fell victim to traumatic experiences in their own homes, from neglectful parents to abuse.

In 1997, one girl in particular, Heaven, kept insisting that she needed to talk to Tarana and finally caught up to her. "[Heaven] had a deep sadness and a yearning for confession that I read immediately and wanted to be no part of," Tarana writes on her website JustBeInc.[85]

Regardless of her hesitation, Tarana listened but couldn't continue the counseling session for more than five minutes.

---

84 "LGBTQ Activism: The Henry Gerber House, Chicago, IL." National Park Service. 2018.

85 Tarana Burke. "The Inception." JustBeInc. 2013.

Heaven was telling her all about her mother's boyfriend, who she referred to as "step-daddy," and what he would do "to her developing body," Tarana writes.[86]

Tarana cut Heaven off in the middle of her confession and guided her to another female counselor, but the look on Heaven's face was one that Tarana says she will never forget.

"The shock of being rejected, the pain of opening a wound only to have it abruptly forced closed again—it was all on her face," Tarana explains.[87] But in that time, she could not find the courage to listen to that girl's pains and help her release the shame.

"I watched her put her mask back on and go back into the world like she was all alone, and I couldn't even bring myself to whisper...me too"

— TARANA BURKE

With Tarana's frustration about being unable to muster the words "me too" to Heaven, she founded the Just Be Inc. non-profit organization in 2006 to show girls of color that they aren't alone in their sexual assault traumas.

---

86 Tarana Burke. "The Inception." JustBeInc. 2013.
87 Ibid.

Tarana Burke thus coined the "Me-Too" movement and shed light on sexual assault victims across the globe.

***

It's inspiring to me that all these incredible people started off just like you and me—they experienced a big event or inspiration that altered their life in one way or another.

Elizabeth Cady wasn't allowed to attend the same conference her husband was attending because she was a woman. Henry Gerber discovered a newfound inspiration to support Gay Rights. Tarana Burke sat across a thirteen-year-old who had the courage she didn't have, of opening past wounds and speaking about personal traumas.

These significant points in each person's life turned out to be one of the best turnovers in history, with their emotional turmoil being the key component.

"The 'Me-Too Movement' started in the deepest, darkest place in my soul," Tarana writes in her blog.

A time that she spent frustrated by her own actions and inability to offer a helping hand to the very vulnerable Heaven, in addition to her own past traumas, turned into an entire wave of women stepping up and saying "me too" in unison for the past decade and many more to come.

I'm so thankful that two hundred years after Elizabeth started the Women's Rights Movement, one hundred years after Henry founded the first Gay Rights organization, and a decade after Tarana started the Me-Too Movement, our society has been positively and directly impacted to this day.

The world needs more domino effects like these, and through your own personal pain and struggles, you *can* create something beautiful even if it doesn't seem like it at that moment. Somewhere down the line, others will be influenced by your words if you find the courage to reach out to others and speak up about your medical error—even if it's just to one person outside your immediate social circle.

After all, it only takes the first domino to fall, in an entire line of others standing in their comfortable positions, to create a massive reaction, and that one domino can be you.

WHEN LIFE GIVES YOU LEMONS

"The true fundamental building blocks of the universe are not particles, but moments in time."

— KHALID MASOOD

I've never heard any successful stories come from a lifetime of ease. How can someone learn to improve their life if it's already as blissful as can be? We *need* events that bring us feelings of discomfort, anger, sadness, frustration, and pain to grow. We *need* resentment, jealously, disappointment, and fear to push us in our darkest moments to create something so impactful that others can be inspired.

I spoke with a long-term medical error survivor named Heather Thiessen, from Saskatchewan, Canada. The positivity that radiated from our phone conversation was so contagious it solidified why I was writing this book—to get more patients inspired by people like Heather.

Heather is a prime example of how open-mindedness and dedication can come hand-in-hand to help you stamp your mark in this world.

At age twenty, as she was pursuing nursing education, Heather was diagnosed with multiple sclerosis (MS) and, ultimately, had to take a disability leave from work.

After getting married, Heather would often find herself in the Intensive Care Unit (ICU), on a ventilator.

"This baffled all my doctors because people with MS don't end up on ventilators," Heather explained.

When her daughter was three months old, Heather's respiratory symptoms continued and she had to be sent to the ICU yet again.

Heather recalls, "I remember a physician coming to my bedside with a tracheostomy tube, which is the device they put in your airway [to make breathing easier], and he put it on the bedside table and said, 'have a good look at this, you'll probably end up with it,' and walked out of my room. I thought, *Well, that's not gonna happen.*"

People often ask me what types of medical events fall under 'medical error' and while the textbook definition of error is a preventable, adverse effect from the care a patient receives, not all events have to be tangible to be errors.

The physician's statement is an example of one no one should say to a patient in the ICU. Textbook definitions or not, society—i.e., you and I—needs to raise more awareness on the importance of health care providers creating emotional safe spaces for patients, and Heather's experience with that physician just doesn't cut it.

Tangent aside, Heather's resilience against the physician's prediction is one to admire. She recovered from the ICU and did not need a tracheostomy.

When her second daughter was nine months old, Heather was diagnosed with a rare, autoimmune neuromuscular disorder called Myasthenia Gravis. With this condition, a person's muscles become extremely weak, especially when their immune system is more compromised. Every time Heather caught a cold, her muscles would give out and she needed to be placed on a ventilator.

During this time, doctors found that her thymus, a gland responsible for maturing our T-Cells, which help us detect foreign invaders in our body, had grown into a tumor called thymoma. She needed surgery to remove the thymoma, which could have allowed Heather to go into remission within five years, but as the years went by, "We realized the surgery didn't work," Heather recalls.

As a result, from 1998 to 2010, she spent "every six months being rushed to ICU with respiratory failure, ending up on a ventilator from two weeks to four months" recovering, and the cycle would repeat itself.

"That was my life for ten years. That's when a lot of my medical errors happened," Heather said.

Due to Heather's many admissions to the health systems and her exposure to latex materials, over time, she learned she had developed an anaphylaxis response to latex.

As health care providers were still learning what materials were and were not causes of allergic reactions, Heather has experienced many anaphylactic shocks from rubber equipment, including rubber stoppers on vials of medication.

Gradually, Heather became an expert on how her body works and reacts, and she became an avid participant in her doctor visits. She starting to ask questions, challenge hospital procedures, and, most importantly, pass on her knowledge to others.

"I told my family, 'You have to speak up for yourself. You have to ask questions. Don't let [health care providers] brush you off—if you don't understand [something], do not leave," Heather told me.

As I spoke with Heather, all I could think was, *How can someone still be so strong after years of pain and medical errors?*

It became clear that Heather's hopeful attitude kept her strong-willed.

It was only after Heathers *many* downfalls and even more comebacks that she began sharing her story.

"I have hope that I *am* going to be part of a better health care system, and that next patient walking in is going to have a better journey than I ever had. That, to me, is what [advocating] is all about," Heather said, explaining why she chose to advocate for patient safety.

She started knocking on doors and actively seeking opportunities from medical administrators, hoping to raise awareness about her medical journey—and it worked.

She approached health conferences and said, "I think you need to hear my story." From then on, they have invited her back to present to various health care professionals, which expanded her network to share her story at many conferences both nationally and internationally.

Similar to the mindsets of Elizabeth Stanton, Henry Gerber, and Tarana Burke, Heather Thiessen approached an unfair situation in her life with a passion to sprout change, and that's all it has ever taken to make a difference in the world.

"If I can change one person's perspective, then I'm doing what I'm doing for a good reason—that's given me a sense of purpose and hope. I'm so excited for the future," Heather said.

THE EYE OF THE BEHOLDER

When life comes along with its unfortunate, random events, we tend to commit the most destructive act of all: we start pitying ourselves, for months, years, and—tragically for some—entire lifetimes.

Dr. Sean Stephenson is an American therapist, world-renown author, and professional motivational speaker from Chicago, Illinois, United States. As I watched his TEDx Talks video, spoken to a room full of prisoners from Ironwood State Prison, I got the slap in the face I was secretly waiting for.

Dr. Stephenson was born with a rare bone disorder that stunted his growth and caused over two hundred fractures by the age of eighteen. In Dave Asprey's interview, he says, "Sneezing would break my collarbone, putting on a pair of pants too quickly would break a femur, coughing would break ribs," not to mention each bone fracture would take weeks to heal.[88] He's had jaw infections where his teeth had to be removed and he now can't chew his own food.

Dr. Stephenson is three feet tall and moves around in a wheelchair.

He needs to be showered and cared for physically by his wife because of his condition, but what makes Dr. Stephenson so empowering is his outlook on someone choosing to suffer vs. someone choosing to live purposefully.

---

88 Asprey, Dave. "How to get over your addiction to pity – – Dr. Sean Stephenson." Dave Asprey. n.d.

In Asprey's interview, Dr. Stephenson says that "pain is inevitable, but what my mom and dad taught me when I was young is [that] suffering is optional. You have a choice to suffer; you have a choice to become addicted to the most addictive substance on the planet...pity."[89]

Even with all the socially constructed pity Dr. Stephenson has experienced in his lifetime, along with the physical, mental, and spiritual battles he's faced in his long journey with the bone disorder, he's spoken in nearly all fifty states in America and in sixteen countries, telling people to stop pitying him and stop pitying themselves.

"The moment you feel sorry for yourself, you're hosed. You are totally and *completely* frozen in potential," he says.[90]

Life *will* throw unhappy things at us every once in a while—it doesn't mean we deserve it, but that's what life is. If the medical error you survived had not occurred, life would throw another difficult event your way in another shape or form because it likes to challenge us, push us past our limits, and inspire us to grow from our discomfort.

---

89 Ibid.
90 Stephensen, Sean. "The Prison of your Mind." 2014.

Dr. Stephenson says to the inmates in the room, "You have to adapt to whatever environment you're in—even if it's prison."[91]

To him, adaption looks like a celebration—a celebration of life.

To me, adaptation is collecting the blocks that life throws at me and using them as tools to pick myself and move on stronger than before.

In my conversation with Donna Penner, we discussed the importance of quotes and the power words can have. A quote she mentioned that stuck with me is, "Life isn't about waiting for the **storm** to pass...It's about learning to **dance in the rain**", by Vivian Greene.

Adaptation is just that: dancing in the miserable, cold rain that life showers us in. If I can't stop the rain from pouring down on me, the least I can do is make do with what I have.

Once we start living and acting in the now, the life we're yearning for, or the life we could have had, stops being on a pedestal. Instead, our quality of life is suddenly found in the little things, like the fact that we have the freedom of speech,

---

91 Stephensen, Sean. "The Prison of your Mind." 2014.

the freedom of volunteering, working, writing, communicating, learning, and growing as individuals.

Our health care system *needs* your powerful voice to help influence how things are run—and after being introduced to Dr. Stephenson, I realized the only things that stand in the way of reaching our full potential are the fears we've created for ourselves.

My fears used to be:

- *I'm just one person, who will listen?* Look at Sean Stephenson, he's just one person too, and millions are listening.
- *I don't have 30 years of experience in health care to have a say in what should be done. Who am I to even talk?* Medical error can happen to anyone at any point, so it's my duty as a lifetime patient to advocate for a patient-centered system.
- *I don't have the resources to reach out to successful people in the field.* All it takes is **one** small action after the other: A phone call, handshake, email, conversation, or Google search to get answers.

I challenge you to make your own list of the fears stopping you from spreading your story and raising awareness. You have the power to stop those fears from ruminating and to turn the page with a fresher mindset.

I'll end this with my favorite quote from Dr. Stephenson's talk that sums up how important our attitudes are:

"If I believe that I am disabled, I would wither up, I would be shy, I would be insecure, I would be afraid, **I would act like I need your help...**but I choose something else. I choose to have words to move this planet."[92]

---

92 Stephensen, Sean. "The Prison of your Mind." 2014.

CHAPTER 9:

STRENGTH AND VULNERABILITY

———

If you look up "strength," the first definition that comes up is "the quality or state of being physically strong,"[93] but don't let that fool you.

Strength is also:

- The influence or power owned by a person
- The emotional or mental qualities needed to deal with difficult events
- The capacity to withstand great pressure

---

93 Merrian-Webster's Learners Dictionary. s.v. "Strength".

Experiencing the loss of a loved one through medical error or having experienced the physical burden of the errors yourself, **and still making it out the other side,** says a tremendous amount about your character and your ability to empower others, however broken you may feel.

Strength is hidden in all of us, but only the ambitious and self-aware make the best use of it—and so can you.

Some think you lose strength when you step down and accept your losses, similar to the act of giving up. However, acceptance does not mean letting "the other team" win—whoever you choose to be "the other team"," whether it's the health care practitioner who was the last person to administer the medical error or all of the Universe itself.

Jon Kabat-Zinn in "Coming to Our Senses: Healing Ourselves and the World Through Mindfulness" says, "Acceptance doesn't, by any stretch of the imagination, mean passive resignation. Quite the opposite. It takes a huge amount of fortitude and motivation to accept what is — especially when you don't like it — and then work wisely and effectively as best you possibly can with the circumstances you find yourself in...**to mitigate, heal, redirect, and change what can be changed.**"[94]

---

94 Kabat-Zinn, Jon. *Coming to Our Senses:* Healing Ourselves and the World Through Mindfulness. 2006.

Likewise, you have the power in *you* to pick up the pieces you have left and build a different reality for yourself—one that inspires other patients to follow your steps and gives you the closure you deserve.

***

I watched a TEDx Talks video of a young speaker, Marieke Poelmann, who lost her parents in an airplane crash when she was only twenty-two.

Being twenty-two myself when I watched her talk, she really put things into perspective for me. We don't always know what we take for granted until it's gone, but Marieke shaped her story into a hopeful one.

She described how just days after the plane crash, she was left to take care of legal work, the bank, brokers, her disabled brother, and suddenly, she felt so much more grown-up than she ever imagined.

"I did all these things I never imagined I could do—I was a lot stronger than I thought," she says.[95]

---

95 Poelmann, Marieke. "Everything around them is still there, dealing with sudden loss." 2016.

As life went on, she had no choice but to move at the pace of life even though she felt like she was condemned or destined to a life full of misery. Somehow though, she found this indescribable power inside of her; a kind of responsibility she owed to her parents. She chose to take over her life and not give it up to the misery she once thought she was condemned to.

In her talk, she brought out a flight safety card that she took from her parent's plane crash in the Libyan desert. What she said next with a chuckle brought the whole room to complete silence.

Marieke said that every time she gets on planes, she scoffs at safety cards. The cards remind her not to hold on to plans and expectations so much, because not everything goes as planned.

In letting go of expectations, you find freedom—freedom to shape your life however you want from that moment on.

Marieke struggled to find a job for many years, and yet in that hopelessness, she still didn't give up. People would say to her, "There are no words to describe what you're going through right now," but Marieke realized that she *did* have words to describe her journey, and she wrote them down.

Her thoughts turned into words and her words into a book, and that journey led her to a career as a freelance journalist and author of many more books.

Marieke left me in tears after watching her talk, and I learned that even in hopeless times, you can still find the strength that was in you all along.

"My beloved parents may have died in an airplane crash. But I didn't—I'm still here," she said.[96]

No matter what your body, mind, or spirit go through, *you* are still here. You survived the crash that was your medical error, you survived the losses you experienced, and through all that, you have the strength and resiliency to get up and leave your mark in this world, no matter how big or small.

I remember a story I was taught in elementary school, and the visualization followed me through the years.

I was in my grade seven religion class, learning about biblical parables. While the lesson in particular doesn't come to mind, my teacher said that if each person in the world ever had the chance to put their problems in a big, giant pile, everyone would want to reach back for their own. So

96 Poelmann, Marieke. "Everything around them is still there, dealing with sudden loss." 2016.

I pictured people coming together from all over the world to drop their problems in the form of sticks in one huge pile and then rushing to get their own sticks back afterward.

The story taught me the importance of counting our blessings even when we experience the lowest of the lows.

It's easy to ruminate about a negative event we experience in our life, but every second ruminating takes us away from the things that can help us grow and move on.

Marieke could have gone down a different path than sharing her story with the world and writing her book. She could have thrown herself a pity party every day of her life, robbing herself of happiness, success, and a sense of belonging in this world. Instead, she knew she wasn't physically affected by the plane crash and could still walk, talk, and write—something not everyone has. She used her skills and everything she didn't lose from her parent's crash to not only cope with her grief but to also inspire many people, including myself—and for just that, I am so thankful.

Many times I doubted myself in writing this book, but every time I came close to even considering giving up, I reminded myself that some people in this world, specifically women, live in political environments that don't allow them to voice their opinions, to write, get educated, and thrive, so

I kept writing. I've realized that the opportunity to write as women is a gift I've been blessed with, and it's not everyone has it.

It's your turn to ask yourself how aware you are of your life's blessings and how you can take advantage of them to create a better life for yourself and inspire others along the way.

TO BE OR NOT TO BE VULNERABLE

In my years at University, I learned so much through my experience away from home.

I met so many amazing people from wildly different cultures, and one of the million things I learned was the importance of vulnerability. This helped me not only find closure in difficult times but also create my own building blocks of success.

Entering University, I never opened up on a deep, personal level with anyone except my family, and that was conditional in itself. This never seemed to affect me at the time because I never knew I lacked vulnerability in the first place.

It's like if someone is a loud chewer but doesn't *know* they're a loud chewer and thinks all is well...until someone else abruptly bursts their bubble and knocks some sense into them.

By the end of the second year, I had a strong social circle. However, also by the end of the second year, I felt lonely. My bubble slowly started bursting when I challenged why I felt so lonely.

I started noticing little things, like how other people around me could be so...unapologetically themselves...with their friends or in public. I would never think to be so 'real' with anyone, even with friends I adore and consider my closest confidants.

It slowly crept up on me: I was scared of vulnerability.

Little by little, through articles, books, podcasts, and self-talks, I worked toward opening up about my mental health and fears to my friends. Lo' and behold, the emotional arm's length distance I once had with my dearest friends faded away.

The amazing part of presenting my real self to the people around me was that they also started to open up to me about *their* fears and all the bits and pieces you find in deeper relationships.

That was not all. The way I interacted with people outside of my social circle changed too.

ASK AND YOU SHALL RECEIVE

By my fourth year of school, vulnerability started becoming easier for me, and I felt my friendships strengthen even more than years past. By that time, I started as a writer for an online magazine called *HerCampus,* a magazine geared toward females on campus that explores themes of women empowerment in all areas of life, from social media to politics to fashion and everything in between.

I wrote all of first semester until exams rolled around in November. For the exam season, I decided it would be helpful to write an article just for first years that incorporated hopeful stories from upper-year students of times they experienced the lowest of lows in their first year but still made it out to the other side.

The catch: I needed fourth year's *personal* stories.

This is where my vulnerability came in handy: I made a post on a few of my university social media groups, asking friends and strangers for help. I asked them to submit their name, year, program, and a story of a time where they were the most stressed in the first year...**the most vulnerable.**

I explained my plans for the article and that I was simply writing it to help first years realize they are not alone in their struggles.

I hesitantly posted my survey, and the results blew me away.

I got stories from students in all years, from all types of programs, with personal experiences that brought me to tears because I wished first-year 'me' could read them and not feel so isolated with academic and personal stress.

I realized I was building a social network with people I barely knew just by asking questions in my most vulnerable state, even though it wouldn't have hurt me to stay quiet. I could have easily changed my article topic and not gone through the discomfort of posting on my school's social media page.

I vowed to myself from that moment on that I would always ask for help when I needed it because People. Are. Human.

They want to feel connected.

Other people *will* break down their defenses once they see that you're opening up to them. They *will* open up about their life as well because they see that you're the real deal—you're not there to hurt them.

Eyes are the windows to the soul, and when people can see through you as someone strong enough to talk about your feelings and struggles **out in the open**, they will trust you to support them through their struggles as well—i.e., they will be given hope.

If you're worried no one will want to hear what you have to say about your medical journey, I'm hoping you'll reconsider. The right people will hear your story and they'll help build the community in which you'll find a louder voice—a voice that will help open up doors for you to make changes in the very settings that left you in pain.

When I was emotionally distancing myself from my friends before I discovered how to be vulnerable, they couldn't magically read my mind and know I was going through a hard time. They couldn't know I was sometimes already so mentally exhausted from school that I would convince myself that my friends didn't even like me to begin with or didn't care what I was going through.

Present me is now yelling, "How could they care if they didn't even know to begin with?"

Whether your version of "they" is family, friends, policymakers, or the entire health care system, make every effort to get your voice heard before you convince yourself "they" simply don't care. I've learned that help won't magically fall into your lap, you *have* to continuously ask for it until you get an answer you're satisfied with.

Sure, some people will act as barriers in your way before you can change how one area of the health care system works, but **the key is not to allow your negative medical experience to make you give up on all of humanity and the people willing to listen and help.**

PROGRAMMED TO CARE

According to the Canadian Patient Safety Institute (CPSI), every thirteen minutes and fourteen seconds, a Canadian patient is harmed in medical settings.[97] If that's the case, we should be hearing about medical errors left and right on the media or in the news, but we don't. If so many patients are being harmed at such a fast rate, medical error should be one of the most prominent conversation starters, and yet it isn't.

This could be for many reasons. It could be due to the stigma around making errors and the fact that many health care providers simply don't publicly talk about their mistakes, or maybe the lack of public awareness on medical error to begin with.

Whatever the reason for the silence over medical error, from 2014 to 2015, the CPSI 2016 report stated that one in eighteen

---

97 RiskAnalytica. "The Case for Investing in Patient Safety in Canada." (2017).

patients was harmed.[98] So one in eighteen people you know or are in your current proximity has been affected by medical error.

That's too many people getting hurt and too little time spent talking about it.

As soon as we start talking about our pain and seeking help from our surroundings, we form a community with others, because after all, human beings are designed to empathize with one another and feel compassion when someone else is suffering.

Dacher Keltner, a professor of psychology from the University of California, has done lots of research in the role of compassion in our lives in an evolutionary sense. Keltner founded the Greater Good Science Center, an organization for the public to help bridge the gap between science and healthy, mindful lifestyle choices. Keltner is an extraordinary speaker on human goodness.

In one of his talks for the Greater Good Science Centre, he explores how humans have evolved to "feel" for other

---

98 "1 in 18 Patients Experience Harm in Canadian Hospitals." Canadian Patient Safety Institute. 2016.

people's pains.[99] Keltner bases this particular talk and most of his research on Charles Darwin, also known as the leading father of evolution. In his famous publications, *The Descent of Man and Selection in Relation to Sex*, Darwin explained that humans have attained survival of the fittest not through selfishness and a "me-first" mentality, but through sympathy.

Darwin writes, "Sympathy will have been increased through natural selection for those communities which include the **greatest number of the most sympathetic members** [and] would flourish best and rear the greatest number of offspring."[100]

In less biological terms, our ancestral communities thrived when they were made up of empathetic and compassionate people.

Keltner explores Darwin's theory further by explaining, "Darwin says sympathy is our strongest instinct; stronger than the maximization of our self-interest."[101]

---

99 Keltner, Dacher. "The Evolutionary Roots of Compassion." Greater Good Magazine. 2012.

100 Darwin, Charles, John Bonner and Robert May. *The Descent of Man, and Selection in Relation to Sex.* Princeton University Press. 1981.

101 Keltner, Dacher. "The Evolutionary Roots of Compassion." Greater Good Magazine. 2012.

Human newborn offspring remain dependent on caregivers (parents) for well over a decade until they can survive on their own. Being caregivers comes naturally to us.

Through his research, Keltner found that as caregivers, we aren't only empathetic to our children and blood relatives, but our brains are literally wired to care for any other human being we see struggling, solely through experiencing the **vulnerability of our offspring**.

Keltner talked about neuroscience labs at the University of California, Los Angeles (UCLA) ran tests to show that once a person feels pain, a part of their brain lights up, and staggeringly enough, if someone else sees that person in pain, the same part of *their* brain lights up as well.[102]

"It's as if we're wired to have the same experiences as other people," says Keltner.[103]

"Fig. 1", an educational channel run by the University of California, presents Keltner discussing his years worth of research focussed on the brain and compassion. Keltner has found that the area in the brain that lights up when people see others in pain is a very ancient part of the human brain,

---

102 Ibid.
103 Keltner, Dacher. "We Are Built To Be Kind." Fig. 1 by University of California. 2014.

called the periaqueductal grey.[104] The periaqueductal grey is also common in other mammals known to have caregiving characteristics.

Vulnerability and compassion are possibly linked, and as human beings, seeing another person being vulnerable triggers us to mirror that vulnerability as well. This fully explains my journey with vulnerability and having my friends and even strangers mirror the same level of vulnerability I exhibited. It explains why I got so many students participating in the mental health article I wrote in my fourth year and why I learned so much about my friends through sharing personal struggles I once hid.

I found closure by bonding with others in my most vulnerable states, and I believe that no matter what anyone experiences, reaching out to others *will* open doors for healing and clarity, both emotionally and mentally.

Sue Sheridan began one of her many successful quality improvement journeys by starting meetups for moms who had children that experienced the same medical error that Sue's son, Cal, had. If Sue had gone quiet and internalized her anger, fear, and pain, she wouldn't have met the seven

---

104 Ibid.

other moms with similar stories and created policy changes that ensured the safety of babies from Kernicterus.

Sue had to practice vulnerability to create a strong community.

I'm not saying you need to make policy changes, but simply making a post on social media or writing an article will do *wonders.*

Let's say out of one hundred people who hear your story, one is sure to reach out to you, and the rest will certainly have their awareness raised on the medical error you survived.

Even just through my writing process, I've learned that people are so much more willing to help you than you think.

Whenever you are ready to accept people's help, take any small effort in sharing your story and making yourself vulnerable, because all it takes is **one** person to change your direction. Maybe you'll bump into someone along the way who has an in with X organization, or knows X politician, or X hospital board of director, and suddenly you are working toward more concrete steps toward a brighter future with patient safety.

CHAPTER 10:

NEW MINDSET

———

It's easy to doubt that one person can create change, but small changes are often needed to create an overall more improved bigger picture. So how can you ensure that you will be successful in your endeavors in creating change?

After all my research, I found one answer to this: There is no one, linear path to success. You just need to stay resilient.

In fact, in health care, successful initiatives might become long, tedious journeys until you find your breakthrough and are suddenly attracting listeners from all over the world, like Donna Penner or Sue Sheridan.

While it's important to tell yourself that you are up for the challenge, this is the time to reflect on the willpower you have, or may need to build, to face your journey head-on.

Let's go back to the research that Dr. Braithwaite, the president of The International Society for Quality in Health Care, has done.

He mentioned in his paper, "Changing how we think about health care improvement" that "[we can build a new approach to change if we] adopt a new mental model that appreciates the complexity of care systems and understands that **change is always unpredictable, hard-won, and takes time. It is often tortuous, and always needs to be tailored to the setting.**"[105]

He believes that anyone, including patients, can make small-scale differences in many ways. Some ways that stand out to me are his ideas of "developing and applying feedback to people involved at every opportunity" and "looking for things going right as well as those going wrong"."[106] Giving feedback and keeping an objective perspective creates a *balanced* perspective.

---

105 Braithwaite, Jeffrey. "Changing How We Think about Healthcare Improvement." *Bmj*, 2018. https://doi.org/10.1136/bmj.k2014.
106 Ibid.

Why is a balanced outlook important? It gives us a stronger foundation for any argument we are trying to make, so we cannot go to an entire health care system, that has traditional policies and little systems basically set in stone, and demand change *just* because we are furious, or hurt, or upset. We need to listen to all sides of the story, assess the system's arguments and view, and take smart steps according to the response we're given.

This is all to say that my favorite method to tackle overwhelming tasks is having trust and patience.

TRUST

"Trust the system." This is the mantra I repeat for myself through tough times.

For me, the system is the Universe or God; to others, the system might be another form of faith, life, a general higher power, or indescribable energy around us—heck, the 'system' could even be the physical, day-to-day life you live in.

Whatever you choose to define the "system" as, having faith that things will work out in our favor helps lessen the pressures of life and gives us the mental adrenaline to "trust fall" into the world.

Trust is also a key component of any relationship, whether it's with friends, partners, family members, colleagues—even strangers. In every interaction we have with others, trust is involved. Store owners trust the public to not come into their stores and steal their products; otherwise, no one would be brave enough to invest in a store. I trust romantic partners to stay loyal and committed; otherwise, I would never want to be in relationships. If you drive, you trust that the person driving next to you won't randomly steer their car into yours; otherwise, you would never drive again.

Trust is everywhere, and yet in all these situations, one person always breaks that trust. One person always shoplifts, breaks someone's heart, or even swerves into your lane because they were too distracted to check their blind spot.

As someone who wants a meaningful life, I choose to trust even when people regularly break that trust. Trust is crucial in your journey with the health care system because not all individuals are "bad" or ignorant or unwilling to listen.

If you have been jaded into being distrustful with the system, whether it's the health care system or the Universe, or life in general, take a step back and learn to open your heart to people around you. Once you do that, you will recognize so many opportunities, resources, and people who will help you raise your voice and stand up to a systematic gap that left you distrustful in the first place.

PATIENCE

"Patience is not simply the ability to wait—it's how we behave while we're waiting."

— JOYCE MEYER

Demanding answers and wanting change is what all patients and advocates in patient safety communities want—but it doesn't always come easy, as we've seen. This goes back to the notion of the health care system being unpredictable. Unpredictability breeds no expectations, because how can you know what an outcome will be if everything is unpredictable?

In his article, Dr. Braithwaite explains the health care system as "a complex adaptive system," meaning that the system's performance and behavior change over time and cannot be completely understood by simply knowing about the individual components[107]. **No other system is more complex:** "not banking, education, manufacturing, or the military", and not even the aviation industry.[108]

---

107 Braithwaite, Jeffrey. "Changing How We Think about Healthcare Improvement." *Bmj*, 2018. https://doi.org/10.1136/bmj.k2014.
108 Ibid.

So as advocates, we cannot go into the system and say, "We want x, y, z changes and we want them now." Change takes time, so instead of setting out on your journey in a hurry, as tempting as it is with all the emotional turmoil you may be experiencing, it will be so much more worthwhile if you take it day by day, resource by resource, small step by small step.

In the meantime, while you are taking your small steps, talk to professionals in the field, reach out to others in the same boat and **keep an eye of out for an "in" with the system.** That "in" can be a CEO that heard your story and wants to implement a bigger change, or a politician willing to hear you out, or even a group of patients who would be interested in creating a support group.

Patience allows for this "keeping an eye out" period because if all you see ahead of you is confrontation, with temporary emotions like anger and frustration blocking your view, you might miss out on amazing people and opportunities on the sidelines waiting for you to pause and ask them for help.

The key is to use both trust and patience at the same time. By trusting that your time will come, you are automatically allowing yourself to take as long as it takes to get to the system change you want. This all seems like rainbows and butterflies, and I understand it could easily be the opposite. Patience does not mean sitting and waiting *with ease.*

In my chat with Donna Penner, she mentioned that even eleven years after her medical error experience, she still sheds tears with every talk she presents to the staff, the public, and students. She still feels the scars of the medical error, and some days simply aren't easy. The key, though, is that she continues to take it step by small step, and in the long run, she has impacted *so many* lives.

The saying, "You don't realize the good old days until they're gone" is such a frightening one for me. We sometimes long for better days ahead, and we like to picture them and put so much focus on what *could* be that we forget about the days we're living in at the moment. The days where you might have impacted someone's day or made a difference in their life, and you haven't taken the time to acknowledge that for yourself and give yourself that boost of confidence and self-love. You may not realize it yet, but if you reflect on your journey thus far, you might remember at least one time where you've spread the word about your story or your need for change and had one person listen. It's all about multiplying that into a bigger picture.

QUALITY IMPROVEMENT

Every field of work needs quality improvement. Society is always advancing, and our systems need to parallel that change and people's demand for growth. With the help of statistics and models, quality improvement in the field of patient safety is the journey to finding the most effective methods to improve health care performance. Going deeper into the specifics, *patient-centered* quality improvement looks at different dynamics in health care and looks for the best set up that encompasses the patient.

But quality improvement is all around us. Agriculture, business, politics, education, law, policing and firefighting, immigration, retail services, and manufacturing all require the constant management and improvement of their systems.

While patient safety is clearly important, we need to ensure that we're applying the same advocacy to these other fields we're surrounded by—the more we practice improving any system, the more skills we gain for effectively improving those most important to us.

For you, that may be patient safety.

This is why patient safety isn't just a field. Much like quality improvement, it's bigger than that; it's a movement, a lifestyle, and a mindset.

"When you're changing the world, it doesn't have to be changing the **whole** world. It can be changing **your** world in a way to make it better." ~ John Paul Flintoff

John Flintoff is a renowned author and highly skilled speaker, and his work revolves greatly around motivating people to help change the world. I've sat through many presentations, heard many podcasts, and read books that aim to help us develop "self-growth", and I really admire the reality he's found in his notion of 'changing the world'.

To him, making a difference in the world doesn't have to be an unattainable goal we set on a pedestal and either wait to achieve when we're ready or wait for someone "more successful" to achieve for us.[109]

You have a unique story and valuable insight to share with the world and with the health care system. Whether one person hears your message or one hundred people do—what matters is you're taking all the micro-opportunities around you to change the system or someone's life with your story.

Raising awareness and inspiring others can be as change-provoking as making health care policy changes.

It took one documentary to help me find enough words on patient safety that filled this book because I felt inspired. I found this sudden need to help change part of *my* world,

---

109 Flintoff, Paul John. "How to Change the World." TEDxAthens. 2012

and I acted on it with the help of many other advocates in the field.

I strongly believe in the power of trying to make the world a better place, whether it's challenging society's traditional ways of doing things or standing up for a neighbor even if doing so won't affect us. When we get into the practice of doing good and making a general difference in our community, we start understanding how to stand up for *ourselves* when life throws us a curveball, including medical error.

Fine-tuning our minds to notice areas of systems that need to be improved is a skill that can be easily developed with practice. More fulfilling is having the passion to be part of a change. Simple acts go a long way, like filling out customer surveys from retail stores to let management know how they're doing as a corporation, to going to parent-teacher interviews and suggesting methods that might benefit your children more in classrooms. These small steps are part of *your* world, but they also help improve situations not just for yourself but everyone else who interacts with the same fields of work.

The beauty of stepping up to change your community is that it has a wonderful butterfly effect—a term first coined in 1972 by Edward Lorenz, a mathematician and meteorologist.[110] He theorized that small changes can cause a momentous effect in the long term and came up with a theory that one single butterfly flapping its wings in one part of the world can start a chain of events that lead to a hurricane formation elsewhere in the world weeks later.

Sometimes when one butterfly takes off, surrounding butterflies follow suit and fly away too. According to the butterfly effect, the force of all these butterflies is just enough to theoretically create a wind so strong it can disrupt the weather in small magnitudes, which causes bigger changes in wind pattern down the line, hence the formation of a hurricane some time after.

Other theorists believe in similar concepts, like John Gribbin, a British science fiction author and astrophysicist. Farnam Street, an educational database, outlines Gribbin's work.

The database highlights Gribbin's book *Deep Simplicity: Bringing Order to Chaos and Complexity,* where he states, "Some systems … are very sensitive to their starting conditions, **so that a tiny difference in the initial 'push' you give them causes a big difference** in where they end up, and

---

110 "The Butterfly Effect: Everything You Need to Know About This Powerful Mental Model." Farnam Street. 2019.

there is feedback, so that what a system does affects its own behaviour."[111]

Making "tiny differences" like telling your neighbor about the reality of medical errors of anesthesia awareness or late cancer diagnoses is equivalent to planting one seed and watching an entire garden eventually grow from it.

You'll be creating your own butterfly effect with your medical error story.

The reason "world changing" doesn't need big initiatives to get the ball rolling is because people will react accordingly to small changes in their environment, just as systems do.

John Flintoff, in one of his TEDxAthens Talks, explains his journey of volunteering in green initiative campaigns after suddenly realizing the depressing reality of the effects of climate change.

He joined many campaign groups hoping to get more people to grow their own food, make their own clothes, and use less polluting transportation methods. But the more he worked for the campaigns, the more he realized that the same people

111   "The Butterfly Effect: Everything You Need to Know About This Powerful Mental Model." Farnam Street. 2019.

kept showing up. "I wanted everyone to change, not just these seasoned campaigners," he passionately explained.[112]

In his quest to save the world from climate change, John then came across a quote by Alastair McIntosh, an environmental activist who said, "It's no good being a campaigner if you're not a good neighbor."[113]

Heavily reflecting on this, John left the campaigns he was a part of to work in his own community, where he had access to a more diverse group of people.

He had a small piece of land where he grew his own fruits and vegetables and one day, he filled a bag full of apples and go door-to-door, offering his neighbors apples.

"That was [a nice way] to get to know people a bit better," John explained.[114]

Six months later, he replicated the same act of kindness, this time with tomatoes. John would tell his neighbors, "Oh dear, I seemed to have grown too many tomatoes. Would you like some?" and they'd take them!

112 Flintoff, Paul John. "How to Change the World." TEDxAthens. 2012
113 Ibid.
114 Ibid.

And just like that, John created a massive difference in his community. He later explained, "I know for a fact that many people in my street that year, for the first time, started growing their own food'."[115]

John's experience is so intriguing because a tiny step in community-building led to an entire movement of growing food in his neighborhood. It definitely wasn't a movement that developed overnight, but the long-term impact of his microsteps made all the difference.

Now imagine the power you have with your story and your suggestions for health care quality improvement. John didn't have to psyche himself out by ruminating on the idea of making a difference with a huge concept like climate change; he just wanted to start a conversation with his neighbors.

Start your own simple conversation with the community around you and watch the butterfly effect take place. Through your passion and commitment to making a difference in the health care system, neighbors, patients, and health care providers alike *will* be moved by your efforts.

Get out there and inspire the next Berenda, because aspiring patient safety advocates are just waiting to hear your story.

---

115 Flintoff, Paul John. "How to Change the World." TEDxAthens. 2012

ACKNOWLEDGEMENTS

This book has been an absolute dream to develop. I've cherished every step.

It's easy to say I wouldn't be where I am today without the unconditional support of my parents and my sister, Benita. Your words of encouragement from Day One kept me going — thank you.

Speaking of Day One, thank you to all my friends back at Queen's for simply just being there when I first started to have an inkling about my book; Britney, Lyra, Laura, Brandy and everyone else who became a part of my writing journey!

Thanks to all the professors, health care practitioners and school administrators who offered their time to give me insight on the world of patient safety. I especially want to thank Dr. Rylan Egan, Kimberly Sears, Dr. David Bowie and the people that made up the QIPEP team for opening my eyes to medical error.

The backbone of this book is made up of all the medical error experiences and powerful messages shared by Sue Sheridan, Donna Penner, Dr. Amy Nakajima, Dr. Danielle Ofri and Heather Thiessen. As well as others mentioned in my book who have taken a stance on the themes of forgiveness, acceptance, courage and strength. Thank you for inspiring me with your words.

I also want to thank the Canadian Patient Safety Institute (CPSI) for the abundance of resources that the public can fall back to in times of need and insight. A special huge thanks to Chris Power, the CEO of CPSI. Our chat reminded me why I was writing this book to begin with.

This goes without saying, but Eric Koester and the Creator Institute---you made this book possible. Thank you for reaching out to Queen's University, and spreading the word about the phenomenal organization that the Creator Institute is. It's true that I felt like I was walking in blindly into this whole journey, but your support, inspiration, entrepreneurship and guidance made it all so much easier. Thanks for everything.

Thank you to Brian Bies and New Degree Press, my publisher. Brian — firstly, thank you for putting up with my frantic messages and questions. I don't know how you did it, but you managed to answer all my "what-ifs" and "hows". Thanks for all your hard and energy work into putting this book together and guiding me through the process.

Even after having developed a book, publishing wouldn't be possible without the help of all my contributors. To family, friends and acquaintances alike, your support and words of encouragement means the world. I feel so lucky to have such an amazing network of supporters around me.

Thanks to my parents, sister and Behrooz Toomezadeh for being my first fans.

Many thanks to my aunt Linda Saber, for taking over promotion and marketing — I appreciate your time. Thanks to Anika, Monica and Hani Saber — and to my grandparents — Alineh and William for all of your love. Thank you to Mimi, Anita, Donna and Bani Sayadof for your support. A special shoutout to my grandparents, Nina and John, for watching over me and pushing me forward all these years. Special thanks to Alen and Nana Sayadof, for all your support and positive vibes — I appreciate you. Thanks to Emma, Mary and Bob Sayadof, for your continued love, as well as to Shamiran Ader and Pierre Derakhshan.

Thank you to my confidants, Britney Jeyanayagam, Laura Chiu, Lyra Hyndrichs, Andris Evans, Margarita Amoranto, Andry Asoh, Tamam Fadhil, Stacey Pereira, Matthew Brooks, Sarah Donegan, Alessandra Schlums, Sam Finkelstein and Shannon Lao. You rock.

Thanks to Pobrina & John Youghana, Mari & Sargis Vardeh, Younatan Koshabe, Lela Schwerin, Anoil Servenous, Karin Lazar and Viyolet Toumasian; to Eileen Yaghoobi, Hedayat Golcheh, Jilbert Gevargizi, Gerald Vartanian, Monika Yadegar, and to Claudia Davidoff. Thanks Deacon Dadway Daniel, Jenny Peera, Nineh Shino, Maryam Hormoze, Violet Malko, Roda Malco, and Albert Malko. Thank you to Mohammad Rasouli, Ghazal Karimi, Nooshin Hosseinnia, Rouzbeh Simyari and Behdad Khafagizadeh. And a thank you to Estrella Melgar, Sharokin Vargeh-Dariush, Cladette Kazar, Raymond Babakhanipour, Kristina Assouri, Joseph Tamaey and Emanouel Ourshano.

Thank you to Eric Keoster, Julia Sun, Hailey Rodgers, Dr. Daniel Woolf, Kwasi Addo, Doris Hahn and Valrie stewart. With special thanks to Dr. Tigalat Shalita and Sabrina Orshan for your tremendous support!

I appreciate you all.

WORKS REFERENCED

———

INTRODUCTION

Cal Sheridan's Journey With Jaundice And Kernicterus |
   CDC". 2018. *Centers For Disease Control And Prevention.*

NORC at the University of Chicago and IHI/NPSF Lucian
   Leape Institute. "Americans' Experience with Medical
   Errors and Views on Patient Safety". 2017 *NORC at the
   University of Chicago and IHI/NPSF Lucian Leape Insti-
   tute.*

RiskAnalytica. "The Case for Investing in Patient Safety in
   Canada." (2017).

Sue Sheridan Video On Patient Safety." Agency for Healthcare Research & Quality. 2012.

CHAPTER 1

"Competency-Based Medical Education." The Canadian
Association of Pathologists (Association canadienne des
pathologistes).

Doty, Michelle M., David Squires, Dana O. Sarnak, Eric C.
Schneider, and Arnav Shah. "Mirror, Mirror 2017: International Comparison Reflects Flaws and Opportunities
for Better U.S. Health Care." TheCommonwealth Fund,
2017.

Marcus, Mary. "Does Your Doctor's Age Matter?" *CBS News,*
2017.

Reason, James. „Human Error: Models And Management".
BMJ 320 (2000): 768-770.

"Residents 'Learn the Ropes' of Competence by Design." Dalhousie University. n.d.

Tsugawa, Yusuke, Joseph P Newhouse, Alan M Zaslavsky,
Daniel M Blumenthal, and Anupam B Jena. 2017. „Phy-

sician Age And Outcomes In Elderly Patients In Hospital In The US: Observational Study". *BMJ* no.357.

World Health Organization. *The World Health Report 2000 – Health systems: Improving Performance.* 2000.

CHAPTER 2

Cooper, Jennifer, Adrian Edwards, Huw Williams, Aziz Sheikh, Gareth Parry, Peter Hibbert, Amy Butlin, Liam Donaldson, and Andrew Carson-Stevens. "Nature of Blame in Patient Safety Incident Reports: Mixed Methods Analysis of a National Database." *The Annals of Family Medicine* 15, no. 5 (2017): 455–61.

KM. "Doctors Who Don't Listen: The Gaslighting Epidemic of Women." Womansats Project, 2019.

Lambda Legal. *When Health Care Isn't Caring: Lambda Legal's Survey on Discrimination Against LGBT People and People Living with HIV.* 2010.

"National Antimicrobial Resisance Monitoring System for Enteric Bacteria (NARMS)." *Centers for Disease Control and Prevention.*

CHAPTER 3

Cooper, Jennifer, Adrian Edwards, Huw Williams, Aziz Sheikh, Gareth Parry, Peter Hibbert, Amy Butlin, Liam Donaldson, and Andrew Carson-Stevens. "Nature of Blame in Patient Safety Incident Reports: Mixed Methods Analysis of a National Database." *The Annals of Family Medicine* 15, no. 5 (2017): 455–61.

Reason, J. "Human Error: Models and Management." *Bmj* 320, no. 7237 (2000): 768–770.

CHAPTER 4

"Anesthesia Awareness Incident Makes Surgery A Nightmare Experience." Canadian Patient Safety Institute. 2016.

"Apology Act, 2009, S.O. 2009, c. 3." Ontario: Search Laws. 2009.

Canadian Anesthesiologists' Society. "Anesthesia FAQ." 2019.

"What Is Anesthesia Awareness?". Canadian Anesthesiologists' Society. 2019.

CHAPTER 5

Friedman, Russell. "The Best Grief Definition You Will Find". *The Grief Recovery Method.* 2013.

Merriam-Webster, s.v. "grief".

PDQ Board. 2017. "Grief, Bereavement, And Coping With Loss". National Cancer Institute (US).

CHAPTER 6

"Anesthesia Awareness Incident Makes Surgery A Nightmare Experience." Canadian Patient Safety Institute. 2016.

Braithwaite, Jeffrey. "Changing How We Think About Healthcare Improvement". *BMJ* 361 (2018).

"I Was Able To Forgive My Sister's Murderer Only By Acknowledging My Own Anger". The Guardian. 2015.

"Patient's Unexpected Death Changes The Way One Obstetrician Thinks All Doctors Should BeEducated." Canadian Patient Safety Institute. 2016.

Wu, Albert. „Medical Error: The Second Victim". *BMJ* 320 (2000): 726-727.

CHAPTER 7

Arimura, Jason, Robert Poole, Michael Jeng, William Rhine, and Paul Sharek. "Neonatal Heparin Overdose—A Multidisciplinary Team Approach to Medication Error Prevention." *The Journal of Pediatric Pharmacology and Therapeutics* 13, no. 2 (2008): 96–98.

Claudia Kalb. "Dennis Quaid: Making Hospitals Safer". *Newsweek*. 2010.

Danielle Ofri,. "Deconstructing Our Perception of Perfectionism." 2015. TEDMED video.

Fahrenkopf, Amy M, Theodore C Sectish, Laura K Barger, Paul J Sharek, Daniel Lewin, Vincent W Chiang, Sarah Edwards, Bernhard L Wiedermann, and Christopher P Landrigan. "Rates of Medication Errors among Depressed and Burnt out Residents." *Bmj* 336, no. 7642 (2008): 488–91.

Steve Kroft. "Dennis Quaid Recounts Twins' Drug Ordeal". *CBS News*. 2008.

"The Quaid Family's Medical Nightmare Video". *Oprah WInfrey Network*. 2009.

Thomas Aloia, "Patient Safety: Should Zero be the Goal?". 2017. MD Anderson Cancer Center.

CHAPTER 8

Asprey, Dave. "How to get over your addiction to pity – – Dr. Sean Stephenson." Dave Asprey. n.d.

"LGBTQ Activism: The Henry Gerber House, Chicago, IL." National Park Service. 2018.

Stephensen, Sean. "The Prison of your Mind." 2014.

Tarana Burke. "The Inception." JustBeInc. 2013.

"The Women's Rights Movement, 1848-1920." United States House of Representatives. 2019.

CHAPTER 9

"1 in 18 Patients Experience Harm in Canadian Hospitals." Canadian Patient Safety Institute. 2016.

Darwin, Charles, John Bonner and Robert May. *The Descent of Man, and Selection in Relation to Sex.* Princeton University Press. 1981.

Kabat-Zinn, Jon. *Coming to Our Senses:* Healing Ourselves and the World Through Mindfulness. 2006.

Keltner, Dacher. "The Evolutionary Roots of Compassion." Greater Good Magazine. 2012.

Keltner, Dacher. "We Are Built To Be Kind." Fig. 1 by University of California. 2014.

Merrian-Webster's Learners Dictionary. s.v. "Strength".

Poelmann, Marieke. "Everything around them is still there, dealing with sudden loss." 2016.

RiskAnalytica. "The Case for Investing in Patient Safety in Canada." (2017).

CHAPTER 10

Braithwaite, Jeffrey. "Changing How We Think about Healthcare Improvement." *Bmj*, 2018. https://doi.org/10.1136/bmj.k2014.

Flintoff, Paul John. "How to Change the World." TEDx-Athens. 2012

"The Butterfly Effect: Everything You Need to Know About This Powerful Mental Model." Farnam Street. 2019.

www.ingramcontent.com/pod-product-compliance
Lightning Source LLC
Chambersburg PA
CBHW071523180526
45171CB00002B/357